Swing By!

Swing By !

ENTERTAINING RECIPES & THE NEW ART OF GATHERING

STEPHANIE NASS

RIZZOLI
NEW YORK

New York · Paris · London · Milan

For anyone
with joie de vivre

Table of Contents

Standing Soirées 85

Introduction

When I was a baby, my parents put my bassinet directly on the dining table when they had guests, so I grew up surrounded by a deep love of hosting and gathering. All my life I have been at greatest peace in the middle of a party, and the instinct to cook for and invite dear friends and loved ones into my home is ingrained in me. When I moved into my own home, a dining table was the first piece of furniture I purchased, and hosting people for dinner has always been my top priority.

Gesamtkunstwerk is a German noun that translates to "total, complete artwork"— and it is widely used to describe opera, which, with its grandiose sets, costumes, and music, incorporates many different art forms to create a larger, greater masterpiece. When I first learned this term as an undergrad at Columbia, however, I thought it was much more applicable to the dinner party, as it encompasses many art forms at one time: cooking, mixology, fashion, music, calligraphy, sculpture, and interior design, among others. Like other art forms, a dinner party offers sensory pleasure, comedic relief, beauty, reflection, and inspiration.

In the same way that a painting is drafted and planned, a spectacular dinner party is the result of methodical organization. The host's initial fantasy must be first loosely, widely defined, then reined in and refined. Checklists, etiquette rules, and budgetary considerations need to be applied.

My art-loving parents were dedicated to nourishment, so I was a child of food and art. My parents constantly hosted in a distinct style that combined their respective interests in the visual and culinary arts. Their Friday-night dinners ranged from Brazilian *churrascarías* with traditional dancers in elaborate costumes to more formal celebrations of the Jewish holidays.

The happiest place in my parents' home is in the kitchen . . . until guests arrive, at which point it is the living room. There guests enjoy appetizers before moving to the dining room, where everyone is seated around a long mahogany table. After dinner, guests return to the living room for additional desserts and more conversation, often in front of a fire.

Food is how my mom communicates love. She taught me that a meal is the most wholly satisfying way to celebrate the ones you love. When you host, you bathe people in gifts of love. When people feel valued, they feel happy; watching my mother create this pleasure for her guests led to my desire to do the same.

I began to cook as a young child, which inspired my nickname and, ultimately, the name of my brand, Chefanie. When I was sixteen years old, I moved to Rennes, France—alone—and while enrolled in the local high school took my first formal

cooking lessons with a seasoned Bretonne chef, Madame Palicot. When I was in college, I began interning—or "staging"— at top restaurants around Manhattan, so I could learn to cook for free. At twenty-three, I began taking night classes at culinary school; by day, I did freelance recipe testing jobs and, on the weekends, started hosting my signature Victory Club suppers.

Victory Club was founded as a roving supper club to bring young professionals together to enjoy food and art, the former inspired by the latter. The evenings were staged in galleries and other spaces dedicated to showcasing artists. The club was covered by the *Wall Street Journal*, *Town & Country*, and *Food & Wine*. The food style of these events was what inspired my catering business. Having created hundreds of parties for celebrities, royals, Forbes 400 brands, and a long list of family members, I understand what it takes to make a spectacular party. What follows are the principles I've defined over many years. Whether you are a novice or an experienced host, these are the tools you need to create memorable, fun parties.

ABOVE: Faux boxwoods sit atop blue and white ginger jars. **OPPOSITE:** Decorative bamboo takes center stage in this place setting, from the flatware, napkin rings, and plates down to ceramic straws and the painted menu.

Principles

In her iconic 1941 oeuvre, *Entertaining Is Fun!*, Dorothy Draper succinctly outlines what you need to "make a party go":

- A hostess who expects to have a good time.
- Some clever touches which give your home a party feeling.
- Friendly guests who come prepared to enjoy themselves.
- Plenty of delicious food, attractively presented.
- Some element of unexpectedness.

This is all correct; however, in my opinion, a party must do more than just "go." Parties should elevate the spirits of everyone in attendance by giving them heaps of positive sensory experiences! Life is too short for bare minimums. Parties should aim to fulfill desires, please all five senses, and transport us outside of our day-to-day ennui.

To become a popular host or hostess to whose home people flock, you must throw events that are as unique and fabulous as you are. Attention to detail makes guests realize how much they were considered and desired. If people feel cared for, they feel happy, and that happiness is what all hosts should strive to create.

I refer to my system as The Chefanie Way. It consists of five principles that have helped me organize and execute sensational parties.

1. The Fantasy

Imagine your fantasy dinner party. This should be specific to you and your personality and should begin as if money were no object. Put pen to paper and start a stream of consciousness exercise that gets you to the heart of your ideal party. No structure . . . just actively conceptualize with energy and passion. Here are some things to consider: In your consummate event, do you prefer to get lost in a sea of people or have rich conversations in a more intimate group of eight to ten? Do you want loud or quiet music? Do you prefer a drawn-out late-night affair or quicker drop-by brunch? The most important part is that this is the party you genuinely want to host. Even if you have an unlimited budget, a party will flop unless you are excited to host it. The guests you choose are likely going to have fun if you are having fun, so you must create an environment where you are happy. Enjoyment—like dread—is contagious. Make sure you are throwing the party you would most want to attend.

2. The North Star

Now that you have the fantasy, it's time to establish a North Star. Boil your fantasy down to one entity; it could be a painting, outfit, song, memory. These examples might seem wildly different, but all of them can be the singular inspiration for a party. All decisions going forward, from napkin folds to wines, should be inspired by whichever one item you have in mind. For example, for a Thanksgiving table one year my North Star image was a plate from the

Isabella Stewart Gardner Museum that had pale blue details among darker motifs; throughout my own tablescape, from the painted menus to the flower arrangements, I followed the color palette of the museum plate and maintained the beautiful balance of colors. For another event, my father's birthday lunch, the North Star was his collection of windup toys; these trinkets were scattered around the table as decor. I chose balloons, party hats, and desserts to match them. Having one clear inspiration ensures the theme and event are cohesive and organized.

3. Escapism

In the same way that a work of literature or theater transports its audience out of the mundane and into another world, a party should be a break from the quotidian. The element of escapism distinguishes a party from a plain dinner. It transports guests to another world and should be a priority as you plan your event.

Depending on the party's fantasy, escapism can be achieved by full floor-to-ceiling decoration—or more subtly with unusual lighting (candlelight), menu choices, arranged flowers, plating techniques, or a specially tailored playlist. A guest may experience escapism, for example, by walking into a flower shop on a winter weeknight to be greeted by cocktails, canapés, and cozy conversation—or when the delicious smells of a thoughtfully seasoned meal seduces someone who usually eats takeout salads.

4. Matchimalism

First heard from UK-based event planner, Fiona Leahy, matchimalism is an attentiveness to things being matchy-matchy. Matchimalism ensures event details all tie together, either literally or conceptually. I love pattern, so I often will use the same pattern on desserts, aprons, plates, and linens.

However, matchimalism can also be more subtle, from coordinating your bamboo flatware to your bamboo earrings or wearing an outfit that matches your floral centerpiece.

As you make decor decisions, check back on your North Star to ensure all party elements align. For example, if your North Star is a wool Pendleton blanket with tribal motifs, minimal matchimalism would include American fare on the menu and table components that match the blanket's graphics. For full matchimalism, use the blanket as a table covering instead of a traditional tablecloth, place a blanket at everyone's chair, wrap pastries in an edible version of the pattern, and ensure the whole table feels like a three-dimensional version of the blanket. When you later get to making your checklist, determine what needs to be sourced.

5. The Zhuzh

The zhuzh elements are the details that wow guests due to their thoughtfulness, rarity, and/

or preparation time. This is the fairy dust that elevates the mundane to the glamorous . . . the "touches of extraordinary" that would not normally exist at a humdrum Monday night dinner. The zhuzh is the difference between serving a baked potato on a paper plate and turning the best heirloom potatoes you can find at the farmers' market into an impressive potato au gratin recipe that you serve on your grandmother's china. Other zhuzhes: using a cookie cutter to shape vegetables instead of doing a rough chop; using an embroidered linen napkin rather than paper; or hanging doughnuts from tree branches rather than serving them in

THESE PAGES: Elements from an event demonstrating the power of matchimalism, from the table linens to the printed cookies, party dress, and the band members' blazers.

their original packaging. The zhuzh is freezing flower petals in ice cubes and bringing peacocks to lunch. The summer that I launched my tableware line in 2019, I invited some friends to try my new designs firsthand. Wanting to zhuzh things up, I asked a farmer friend from Connecticut to bring his peacocks and baby goats to roam around our lunch.

In terms of recipes, zhuzh recipes are the ones that require more effort; they are labors of love. Zhuzh wines are the ones you've been saving to savor in the right company. On the table, linens and china both add zhuzh. If you're deciding between linens and china, linens are generally less expensive but more likely to stain. As tableware is my passion, I collect both but would sooner opt for neutral china and have multiple patterns of statement linens to rotate.

The juxtaposition of old and new creates a special zhuzh: It puts the party within a wider history of events, celebrating tradition. This inclusion of old-new elements can extend beyond the decor: adapt Grandma's cookie recipe for a gluten-free diet or print an antique rug on a cake, as my company is known to do! If you are using freshly cut flowers, there are few things as beautiful as seeing them in an antique vase.

Antique stores (and the online equivalent) usually have gently worn hosting accoutrements that are often made by hand—the opposite of boring, mediocre mass market options. Secondhand shopping often saves money. After those channels are exhausted, supplement with new pieces. The collection you acquire over time will reflect your personality and establish your hosting identity.

A Chefanie place setting with matchimalist elements. Zhuzh factors include the flatware, with silver-tassel handles, and the silver-plated drinking glasses.

The Checklist

Now that the principles are established, it's time for the checklist. The checklist will keep you organized and prevent overlooking any important details. Embellish yours by mentally strolling through the evening—attuned to the smells, sights, tastes, sounds, and textures at each stage. Different parties will vary in their needs. Make sure that all elements connect back with the initial fantasy. The checklist will bring the North Star down to Earth, and it is where things become realistic.

Here are things to consider when creating your checklist, in the order that I've found makes the most sense:

1. Budget

Identify the amount (or range) you are able to spend in order to stretch and creatively work within it.

2. Venue

If your budget is limited, the event can be held somewhere with free access (a home, a public park, a friend's yard); if your budget is more expansive, the venue can be inspired more directly by the fantasy (a hotel ballroom, a museum, a bowling alley). If the former, you will need to consider weather, the capacity, and how the event can be decorated to tie back to the North Star.

3. Date

Consider the soonest you can host the event, or plan around an unmovable milestone like a birthday. Target a realistic date in which everything needed for the party can be acquired. Don't drag it out, though, or momentum will be lost.

4. Guest List

When you're determining the guest list, think carefully about the connections you would like to build among your guests and who will get along. I like to invite a mix of people I know well and those who I wish to know better, and I include some outsize personalities with good listeners. Your guest count depends on the vibe of your party fantasy and the size of the venue you select, which depends on the budget you have available.

5. Invitations

The invitation is the first impression guests will have of the party. It sets the tone in terms of formality. It should explicitly outline the host, date, time, place, occasion, dress code, and RSVP deadline. It should make reference to the food that will be provided, such as "Join us for dinner" or "Stop by for nibbles."

It should be personalized to some extent—even if it's merely a name typed onto a Paperless Post envelope. My favorite way to personalize is by

Long Languid Lunch

Summer Quiche
Zucchini Carpaccio
Chicken Paillard
Corn Salad
Tomato Salad
Haricots Verts
Blueberry Pie

Salsa Verde
Roasted Potatoes
Rainbow Asparagus
Heirloom Carrots
Chinoiserie Cakes

Richmond, Virginia

Martini Me
Martini Menu
Martini Menu
Martini Menu

Menu

Cupid's Kiss Cockta
It Girl Salad
Steak with He
Chocolate

MENU

Chestnut Soup
Roast Potatoes
Haricots Verts
Braised Cipollini Onions
Beef Tenderloin
Duck Confit
Dessert Buffet

Menu

Caprese Cooler
Sicilian Slice
(with assorted toppings)
King Midas Slice
Roasted Broccolini
Rainbow Cookies
Red Gingham Cake

Waterm
Gi
Emerald C
Veggie Bo
Bouquet of F
Key Lime Pie Popsic

ME

Follow the Sun
Grilled Sunflower
Roasted Vegetables
Seed-Encrusted Tuna
Sautéed Sunflower Leaves
Almond Cake

Menu

STARBOARD
JAR-CUTERIE
AVOCADO BOATS
CUCUMBER SANDWICHES
VER COOKIES

MENU

Gardener's Spritz
Spring Rolls
Harvest Salad
Chicken Paillard
Cookies
Cake

ASIAN

Farfalle with meat
Ravioli and Pesto
Cacio e Pepe
Sautéed Greens
Rigatoni Cannolis

Always have enough appetizers so that someone could feel totally satisfied with just hors d'oeuvres. At a minimum, plan for three hors d'oeuvres per person.

Dietary restrictions are very common these days. If you are serving a buffet or family style, have enough dishes so that any guests who are gluten- or dairy-free or vegan won't leave hungry or dissatisfied. For a party of twelve, I might serve a vegan soup, two proteins, two vegetables roasted in olive oil, and one gluten-free starch.

If you are plating everything, make it appealing to as many diets as possible, and be careful to note each guest's dietary restrictions as they RSVP.

Be cognizant of how many ovens, pans, and pots you have.

handwriting each name, but if you hate your handwriting, you can hire a calligrapher.

Invite the most outgoing, entertaining guests to come ten minutes early to get the party started and set the tone.

As you begin collecting confirmations, you can start abstractly thinking about seat assignments and dietary restrictions. Seating is very important for all types of "matchmaking," whether it be related to romance, friendship, or business.

6. Menu

As you create your menu, be sure you will make maximum use of your oven: it is more forgiving than the stovetop and really does so much of the work for you.

I take advantage of my many kitchen appliances. My Thermomix multicooker is really the Rolls-Royce of appliances because it makes perfect saffron risotto at the touch of a button! In addition, it blends pesto and soups to velvety smoothness. Good appliances are investments in many ways, for example eliminating the need for extra helpers.

Fastidious preparation can also obviate the need for additional help: many dishes can be made ahead and reheated beautifully.

To gain familiarity with recipe nuances and timing, make each recipe at least twice before showtime. Practice makes perfect.

The menu should be tied back to the North Star and fantasy and, most important, it should be delicious.

7. Dessert

Some people might consider this part of the menu, but for me, dessert needs to be its own category. In choosing a dessert, you determine the taste that guests will have on their tongue when they depart your transportive fantasy event. When you host, desserts can be the pinnacle zhuzh.

Do you have the capacity to bake a dessert? A standard cake can be made a few days in advance of the event if properly stored; sugar is a preservative.

Store-bought and homemade cakes alike can be elevated in minutes with a sprinkle of gold leaf, addition of edible flowers (dried or fresh), or the application of Chefanie Sheets.

Are there any birthdays among the guests? You'll need candles (and matches).

At the end of dinner, I always come around with warm cookies on a tray to surprise and delight—a guaranteed crowd-pleaser that I learned from Shelly Fireman at Café Fiorello. Cookie dough is easy to prepare in advance, and my quarter-size cookies take only minutes to bake. Beyond the cookies, I put out little bowls of pretty sweets to encourage guests to linger.

8. Source Ingredients

Seasonal vegetables are more sustainable and often less expensive.

Fish should be purchased no more than one day before the event. Always buy from a trusted fishmonger and smell it; fresh fish should be virtually odorless.

Butchers are magicians and can facilitate the cooking of meat at your party. Have the meats butchered for you whenever possible. For example, if you are making chicken schnitzel,

let the butcher pound the meat to the desired thickness; if you are making tenderloin, let the butcher trim any excess fat. When it comes to roasting chicken or turkey, individual pieces cook faster and more evenly. They also make for a more elegant presentation and require less work in the kitchen at the time of serving. Ask the butcher to break down the bird for you.

Buy what is within your budget, but "splurge" on the most expensive ingredients that you can afford. If your budget is limited, splurging on items such as high-quality eggs and butter can make an enormous difference in the quality of your dishes without breaking the bank. If you have a bigger budget, a splurge on white truffles can take a dish to a whole other level of luxury that your guests won't forget. Ingredients are critical to the enjoyment of food.

Most of the time, don't bother with fresh pastas. Many chefs agree they are finicky and not as consistent as dry pastas, though stuffed pastas like ravioli and tortellini are the exception. If you make your own pasta, use a decorative mold or shape that relates to the North Star.

In general, always keep a stocked freezer (puff pastry, piecrust, croissants, cookie dough) and a stocked pantry (nuts, dried fruits, chocolates, preserves) in case of unexpected guests.

9. Drinks

A full bar for cocktails is lovely but requires a constant pair of attentive hands. If you have a cohost, this job might be delegated to him or her, or, if budget allows, hiring a bartender would make sense. Original cocktail names, garnishes, and glasses should be contemplated as a no-cost whimsical detail.

There are so many directions for a cocktail garnish, and many can be prepared in advance: ice cubes with edible flowers, made from frozen fruit juice, or made in uniquely shaped molds; toothpicks of olives, maraschino cherries, or colorful gummy candy like sour lips; and citrus or other fruit/vegetable slice garnishes. If I have enough bandwidth, I might do a more involved garnish like smoke!

Most of the time, I prefer to keep drinks simple with a pre-batched cocktail or a wine plan: sparkling wine on arrival, white wine with the first course, red wine with the second course, and a return to champagne at the end. Waters and non-alcoholic options are imperative too; sparkling and still waters should be your baseline.

10. Music

Event music should tie back to the North Star too. Music is felt before any food or beverage is even consumed. The volume, message, speed, or era of what you play communicates the vibe of your event earlier than, and as much as, the provisions.

Holiday parties can go in all kinds of directions. Pop-star renditions of holiday ballads will create a different tone than Tchaikovsky's *The Nutcracker.* The former feels younger and looser, the latter more traditional. Both can be used in irony as well, depending on the rest of the party. For example, at an "ugly sweater party" among college friends in NoLIta, playing *The Nutcracker* is cooler than someone playing the same in a staid apartment uptown.

When planning a recent backyard birthday party, where the North Star was a scrapbook of the guest of honor's life to date, I hired a Beatles cover band. Sure, they were dressed in chintz blazers on an April afternoon, but the familiar sounds put guests at ease. Some guests sang along and danced. It was comfort music, matching the era of the scrapbook as well as the food and guest list.

TIP: WHICH MUSIC IS BEST?
Live music is the best, but if that's not an option, music played on a vinyl record player is superior to what comes out of your Bluetooth speakers. That said, vinyl records have to be flipped or switched, which requires attention. A cell phone playlist is easiest.

11. Home Decoration

What differentiates a space from ordinary to a party venue is accomplished with some work. When hosting at home, think about ways to make your exterior sing "welcome." Whether it is your front door or gates to a long driveway, the entrance should be dressed in party attire. It's the absolute first impression upon arrival. A wreath or balloons connote celebration and, on a practical level, identify the venue for guests who have not previously visited. There is a wide range of options for this—from a beautifully handwritten sign that says "party here" to a full-on fresh flower frame around a door.

12. Table Decoration

A very important part. Much more on this on page 27.

13. Smells

Often an overlooked aspect of a party's ambiance, smells are important and are something to consider carefully ahead of an event. Are you

only scenario in which I would not prioritize comfortable chairs is for a dance party.

15. Temperature

Many people are very sensitive to temperature and guests should be comfortable enough not to notice. Anticipate the outdoor temperature and solutions to deal with it. If it's hot and muggy, turn on the air-conditioning hours before the party. If it's a winter party where late-night dancing will ensue, heat the room and then remember to lower the temperature.

16. Personalized Elements

Every guest's name should appear in at least one place at the event, most typically on place cards and most charmingly if written by hand.

17. Outfit

This always ends up last on my list, but don't forget to rise to the occasion through your own garments and accessories. Do not be a martyr and sacrifice your own appearance after you put so much effort into the affair.

preparing fish or frying chicken? Those are generally considered unpleasant smells. Will you use lemon juice, fresh air, and scented candles to eliminate the odor? Do you want the space to smell like sautéed onions, freshly baked bread, mulled wine? I prefer these natural smells to any scented candles. If you don't want food smells, utilize fresh flowers, incense, potpourris, scented candles, diffusers, and open windows.

Do you have pets? Make sure they are freshly brushed, groomed, and smell-free, and be sure that hair is removed from all surfaces and seating.

14. Chairs

Especially important for seated dinner parties. Before you host guests, make sure you yourself can withstand at least ninety minutes in your dining chairs. If they would benefit from additional cushioning, procure pillows. The

The crescendo

Finally, we come to the crescendo. Once all the planning is done, this is how the event will optimally unfold and in the order that it will happen. It puts the checklist into action and brings it to life. The crescendo ensures that you're ready to go when the first guest walks in the door: the wine is chilling, there are wine glasses and a bottle opener within easy reach, and there is a stack of freshly pressed cocktail napkins ready to be used. The crescendo sets you up to enjoy your party as much as your guests will.

The following party preparation takes place the week or day of the event, beginning with elements that can be done farthest in advance:

Set the Table
(up to 1 week ahead)

If possible, there are many benefits to setting the table in advance. While those of us living in tight quarters use the dining table for multiple functions, including remote work, and might not be able to forfeit it for one week, setting the table ahead of time does not diminish its ultimate impression, and there's no reason to wait until the last minute; unlike fresh produce, the tablecloth will not wilt. In addition, you can edit your floral plans based on how the linens, china, and more look together.

The tablecloth is the foundation of the table— select a bold tablecloth and eliminate wrinkles. Layers raise a mediocre table to a fabulous one. This means, in addition to the tablecloth, chargers and/or place mats, plates, napkins, menus, and place cards, as well as low flowers and tall skinny candles.

When you set the table, there's a beneficial order of operations. Lay the place mats or chargers, glassware, and flatware first. This way, you know what space you have to work with for the centerpiece. A common mistake when setting the table is putting the blade of the knife outward; the blade of the knife should always face inward, toward the plate.

Table flowers should never be too high—a maximum of shoulder height. If you are using garden flowers, be sure you're familiar with how long they last in water. Buying potted plants instead of cut flowers is a more sustainable option for flora, and they can be replanted in your yard or given as parting gifts. If you are on a tight budget, you might purchase flowers from your grocery store. If you have a big budget, perhaps you'll enlist a local floral designer to create magic that corresponds to your North Star. Most flowers can be arranged the day before the event. Hydrangeas need to be snipped day-of.

The tallest element on the table should be thin taper candles. You can also use low tea lights to light guests from below. Candlelight flatters guests as well as the food. If you have enough candles to use instead of lightbulbs, concentrate them in the center of the table. It draws people inward and closer—we're all drawn to fire in darkness.

Small snacks on the table allow for munching in between courses and double as decor. Nuts, colorful candies, and dried fruits can go in pretty bowls in the center of the table. Chocolate turkeys are a Thanksgiving classic at each place setting. Consider unusual but interesting vessels to hold some of these small decorative snacks, such as miniature bird cages; their little doors allow guests to interact with the table itself. Other items for the centerpiece might be low sculptures or other tchotchkes. Salt and pepper shakers can be communal or individual but cannot be forgotten. Keep your eyes open for interesting pieces when you visit thrift stores, yard sales, or antique stores.

Depending on how much help and/or room you have, bottles of wine and water pitchers can go on the table. This allows guests to help themselves. Alternatively, you can pour beverages.

Personalize each place setting. A place card is traditional and elegant. An alternative customizable object is surprising and can double as a parting gift. Some examples over the years have been chocolates, lemons, oranges, cookies, bread rolls, shells, and embroidered linen napkins.

Statement napkins can be collected and reused. Embroidered linens will always be more expensive than printed cotton, but they enhance the place setting exponentially. With a little practice, you can also embroider napkins yourself. If you are including a bowl in your place setting, you might put the napkin to the left of the flatware; just make sure to abide by the formality that the folded side of the napkin is nearest to the plate. Napkin rings should be added on a case-by-case basis; try a napkin ring with your napkin and see if you like it.

Hand-painted menus add another personal touch and texture, as well as zhuzh. Once one is made, I have enough printed for each place setting. When one chooses calligraphy for the invitation, ceremony, and menus, it creates cohesion. Depending on your budget, professional illustrators and calligraphers can do this work, but if your budget is tight, a relative or friend might be able to help as well.

What makes a table come alive is the people around it. Seat guests close enough to one another so that the table feels full.

Prepare Parts of the Meal
(up to 3 days ahead)

The meal preparation can be done in stages. Do the following in advance:

- Make soup
- Make cake (many can be made ahead)
- Clean and chop fruits and vegetables
- Prepare any dishes that require marination or long-term cooking, such as confit duck legs or brisket
- Make cookie doughs and portion on baking sheets

My earring collection was inspired by a need to get dressed quickly. Putting on some baubles always makes me feel "ready," even if I'm greeting guests after cooking in front of a hot stove.

Finally, don't forget to take care of your hair. My mom, the consummate hostess, always makes a 3:30 p.m. hair appointment before guests arrive at 7 p.m. By that time, her food preparation is complete, with only some reheating to be done before serving. Styled hair is a personal zhuzh and signals the specialness of the occasion.

Write Seat Assignments

I always save this final step for the end, as people cancel at the last minute. While I do plan the place card medium (cards, candies, fruit, etc.) and seating arrangements ahead of time, I wait to actually personalize until moments before the event begins.

Light the Candles

While unscented candles on the table and in the entrance (so as not to overpower the food) and a scented candle in the powder room should be placed in advance of the event, light everything just before the first guest enters. Then, get the music going.

The more that is done in advance, the more you can enjoy your party stress-free.

Finishing Touches
(day of)

Tidy up

The foyer, dining room, and living room are where guests will spend most of their time, so make sure those areas are spick-and-span. However, often neglected is the powder room: make sure to light a scented candle, lower the lighting, empty the garbage can, refresh the hand towels, replenish the toilet paper, and set out a box of facial tissues.

Dress Up

Make sure that your outfit is ironed and ready to be slipped on just before guests arrive.

ABOVE: Dressed to coordinate with tartan cakes, cookies, and doughnuts at a pop-up event in Manhattan's SoHo neighborhood. **OPPOSITE:** When possible, wearing a festive dress sets a celebratory mood—as does having wine open and ready to enjoy when guests arrive!

The Parties

Seated Suppers

The seated dinner party is the pinnacle of civilized society. My years of catering have given me an arsenal of well-honed tricks to facilitate hosting a seated supper. First and foremost, when planning the menu, let the oven be your best friend . . . it will do so much of the work for you, which includes baking side dishes (often all at once). The stovetop can be trickier, requiring more constant stirring and attention to simmering pots. Moreover, many dishes can be mostly made ahead, requiring only some quick heat before serving.

Among the serving styles, plated presentation is the most elegant option but also requires the most hands-on labor. Family style presentation, on the other hand, is intimate and cozy.

For the tablescape, differentiate your special gathering from an ordinary evening with a tablecloth. Setting the table should be an expression of creativity. On a practical level, ensure you have enough cutlery for everything you're serving. And as a reminder about place settings: forks go on the left (a trick for remembering this—"fork" and "left" are both four-letter words). Each knife and spoon goes on the right (all five-letter words). Take my advice: you will not have time to wash the salad forks between the first course and dessert—although you should start the evening with an empty dishwasher, if you have one. Plan your menu based on the tableware that you have.

Draw guests to the table by lighting tons of candles in the middle of the table. The flickering light is a welcome escape from our daily load of digital blue light from cell phone screens and light bulbs. Moreover, these flames illuminate faces in the most flattering way, which is really the point of all this anyway. Dot the rest of the table with flowers, short candles, fruits, candies—all below the shoulder line so as not to disrupt conversation.

Consider a dessert bar to cap off your seated supper: the languid pace at which guests make selections means they linger at the table for a longer time. Comfortable dining rooms chairs help too!

Menu

Chestnut Soup
Roasted Potatoes
Haricots Verts
Braised Cipollini Onions
Beef Tenderloin
Duck Confit
Dessert Buffet

Alpine Affair

During college, I studied German, spent a summer in Berlin, and traveled around the German-speaking world from Austria to Switzerland. I fell in love with the preparations of game meats and the cheerfulness of traditional costumes. I tasted the *glühwein* (mulled wine) at *weinachtmarkts* (Christmas markets), visited winter lodges in the Tyrolean mountains, and chomped on *lebkuchenherzen* (heart-shaped ginger spice cookies). Captivated by my memories, I decided to design a party where German Alpine landscapes were the North Star.

This party took place at the foot of Aspen Mountain, during ski season, but it can be recreated in in a shoebox New York apartment too. I was specifically intrigued by the overlooked beauty of the forest floor during winter. To celebrate it, I covered

A place setting inspired by an Alpine forest floor. The decoration on the cookie at each place setting incorporates traditional Tyrolean motifs. The turf table covering, green glassware, antler place card holders (from Chefanie), and wood chargers add to the woodsy feel.

the dining table in moss (affordably purchased online or at a craft store) and then decorated the center of the table with natural elements one might find on a winter walk in the woods: antlers (purchased on Etsy); acorns, pine cones, and feathers (collected on a winter walk near my parents' house); and mushrooms (sourced at the grocery store). The rest of the tableware complemented the colors of those elements: brown, white, and green. The zhuzh came from candles, crisp napkins, and careful arrangements of flora. Burning a pine-scented candle, coupled with the smell of a simmering Hot Toddy, further helped transport guests.

The menu was warming and rich, which is exactly what is craved in the dead of winter! Chestnuts are a special winter ingredient; puréed into hot soup, they are hearty and delightful. Meltingly tender duck confit is perfect at this time of year. Everything was served family style except dessert, which we laid as a buffet. I took liberties to create American interpretations of German sweets: an apple galette was our answer to *apfelstrudel*, and colorful sugar cookies were our answer to *lebkuchenherzen*.

ABOVE AND OPPOSITE: Nestled at the base of Aspen Mountain, the tables looked right at home. The color palette of green, brown, and white ties to the North Star concept of the forest floor that inspired the party.

ABOVE AND OPPOSITE: Mixing different Chefanie elements in the same Green Leaf pattern makes for a fun and fresh table. In this instance, a tablecloth is heavier than a scalloped-edge place mat because the pattern extends all over.

HOW TO MAKE
The Forest Floor (on the Table)

1. Measure your table and purchase enough dried moss to cover it.

2. Lay dried moss flat on the table (using double-sided tape if it will not stay down).

3. On top of the moss, set the chargers or place mats, glassware, and flatware for all of your guests, so you know how much space you have to play with for centerpiece decor.

4. Alternate the table decorations: antlers, flowers, candles, acorns, pine cones, and feathers. It's not a scientific process, but use your best judgment on the crowding of props. If I'm ever unsure about prop density, I whip out my cell phone camera and evaluate the centerpiece through this lens; it's like a second set of eyes.

RIGHT AND OPPOSITE: Using food dye, we printed this graphic directly onto heart-shaped sugar cookies. Over the years, we have printed many different patterns, logos, and pictures with this method. My signature wicker basket is the ideal carrier for these confections, as its sturdiness prevents breakage.

Beggar's Purses

Inspired by an appetizer of the same name from the iconic 1980s New York haunt, the Quilted Giraffe, this version is quicker to prepare and gluten-free. Moreover, my cousin told me each morsel was $50 apiece in 1990; the price is more reasonable when you make them yourself. The decadence here is in the quality of ingredients, which are nice to splurge on, if possible, for a special occasion. While the caviar is optional, it adds an extra zhuzh to the dish.

Makes 8 parcels; serves 8

INGREDIENTS

2 ripe avocados, halved, pitted, and peeled

1 teaspoon freshly squeezed lemon juice

1 teaspoon kosher salt

8 slices smoked salmon (about 16 ounces)

8 whole chives

2 ounces caviar (optional)

DIRECTIONS

1. In a small bowl, mash the avocado with the lemon juice and salt.

2. Lay out the slices of smoked salmon on a work surface. Place a dollop of mashed avocado in the center of each slice.

3. Gather the edges of the salmon slice together, so you can form a ruffle at the top of the avocado dollop. Tie the chive around the ruffle to secure the purse. Place a dollop of caviar in the top of the ruffle, if using.

Spiced Hot Toddy

Before anyone even has a sip, this cocktail does much legwork in the way of setting the tone for a wintery party. Its preparation's fragrance connotes warmth. It's an American twist on German Glühwein—with apple cider mixed in. Moreover, I love drinking this even when there's no sign of a party—it's remedial during cold and flu season.

Makes 8 drinks

INGREDIENTS

5 cups red wine like a red German Pinot

1 cup apple cider

2 teaspoons ground cinnamon

2 teaspoons ground ginger

2 teaspoons honey

2 apples, cored and sliced into ¼-inch-thick pieces

8 cinnamon sticks

DIRECTIONS

1. In a medium saucepan, combine the wine, apple cider, cinnamon, ginger, and honey over medium-high heat. Use a wooden spoon to stir until the honey dissolves, then let simmer over medium-low to allow the flavors to meld, about 20 minutes.

2. You can keep this cocktail warm over the lowest simmer all evening, but make sure to keep adding wine, cider, and spices if it starts to evaporate.

3. For each serving, ladle the drink into teacups and garnish with an apple slice and cinnamon stick.

Duck Confit

In my family, we have a tradition of cooking duck for special occasions. This began with my grandmother's legendary roast duck. Full credit for this recipe, however, belongs to my mother, who is the master of family holidays, from the decor to dishes. The duck here is cooked in the fat rendered from the legs, so it is less fatty than a traditional confit. This fall-off-the-bone-tender duck delights even the most jaded of duck eaters. I know it because people take second helpings—and sometimes even thirds, so scale up the recipe based on your audience.

Serves 8

INGREDIENTS

8 duck legs

2 tablespoons kosher salt

2 ½ tablespoons ground coriander

Mom's Dry Rub (1 teaspoon each of dried minced garlic, dried minced onion, freshly ground black pepper, freshly ground pink pepper, dried parsley, sweet paprika, dried orange peel)

Cloves from 2 heads garlic, peeled

DIRECTIONS

1. Preheat the oven to 250°F.

2. In a small bowl, mix the salt, coriander, and Mom's Dry Rub. Carefully poke the duck skin and all fat pockets with a sharp knife, but do not puncture the meat itself. Rub the seasoning all over the duck legs.

3. Place the duck legs in a Dutch oven, skin side down, with the garlic cloves and 2 tablespoons water. Cover and transfer to the oven.

4. After 2 hours, use tongs to gently flip the legs. Return, covered, to the oven. After another 2 hours, check the legs. If tender, the meat should be easily pierced with a paring knife. If not, return to the oven and check on them every 10 minutes, until they are done. Transfer the duck legs to a plate.

5. To save the fat, strain the remaining contents of the Dutch oven through a fine-mesh sieve into a bowl.

6. To serve the duck legs same-day: Place the legs on a baking sheet, skin side up. Roast in the oven at 450°F for 20 minutes, until the skin is caramel brown and crisped. Brush the reserved duck fat on the legs when they come out of the oven.

To serve within 1 month: Let the duck legs and duck fat cool. Place the duck legs in an airtight container and pour the duck fat over them. The legs should be completely submerged. Refrigerate for up to 1 month. When ready to cook, gently remove the legs from the hardened duck fat, place on a baking sheet, and roast in a 450°F oven, skin side up, for 20 minutes.

7. Serve the duck with any or all of the following: sour cherry jam, roasted fingerling potatoes, kale sautéed in rendered duck fat, roasted cipollini onions, chestnuts, and cornbread.

THIS PAGE: I recreated this Alpine meal in my tiny one-bedroom apartment in New York City. It was escapist fun for all the guests.

Apple Galette

This open-faced apple dessert is what I would generally call a no-recipe recipe, but for the sake of this book, a recipe follows. Much of the beauty here derives from the arrangement of the apples, so take extra care to slice them neatly. You can also mix different colored apples, so the skins offer pretty contrast. I always think Honeycrisp are the most delicious, though. If you are short on time, store-bought pie dough can be used.

Serves 8

INGREDIENTS

PIE DOUGH

3 cups all-purpose flour, plus 1 tablespoon for rolling

1 ½ teaspoons kosher salt

12 tablespoons (1 ½ sticks) unsalted butter, cold

¾ cup cold water

FILLING

3 tablespoons light brown sugar

1 teaspoon ground cinnamon

½ teaspoon kosher salt

2 teaspoons freshly squeezed lemon juice

3 to 4 Honeycrisp apples, cored and sliced into pieces, each apple's slices kept together

1 large egg, beaten

1 10-ounce jar salted caramel (optional)

Vanilla ice cream, for serving

Whipped cream, for serving

DIRECTIONS

Make the pie dough:

1. If using store-bought pie dough, skip this step. To make the dough, combine the flour and salt in a mixing bowl. Then incorporate the butter with a pastry cutter or fork until little balls form. Slowly add the cold water and mix until a large ball of smooth dough forms. Wrap the dough in plastic wrap, and refrigerate for at least 1 hour and up to 1 week.

2. Once ready to use, sprinkle a clean surface with flour. Roll out the pie dough to ⅛ inch thick to form a circular shape. Place on a parchment-lined baking sheet.

Make the filling and assemble:

1. Preheat the oven to 400°F.

2. In a small bowl, combine the brown sugar, ground cinnamon, kosher salt, and lemon juice.

3. Place the groups of apples, peel side up, on the rolled-out dough, leaving about a 1-inch border of dough. Sprinkle the apples with the sugar-cinnamon mixture.

4. Fold the edges of the pie dough toward the apple slices. Brush the folded edges with the beaten egg.

5. Bake until the crust is golden brown and the filling is bubbly, about 45 minutes.

6. Brush caramel sauce all over the apples. Bake another 2 minutes.

7. Serve warm with vanilla ice cream—or the German way, *mit Schlag* (with whipped cream).

Menu

Gingertini

Caviar Swans

Lamb Chops

Vegetables

24 Karat Carrot Cake

Gilded Feast

One of my best friends is a font of creativity. Years ago, he brought gold leaf to a New Year's party and meticulously applied it to many of us, adorning us in this festive metal. Inspired by the celebratory effect of this long-ago party trick, I wondered what would happen if I extended the gold theme to an entire party. When done poorly, gold is tacky. However, when done right, yellow gold is warm, glowy, universally flattering bliss. The sparkle itself distinguishes a special occasion from everyday humdrum; it allows guests to escape their worries and bask in the pleasures of life, which is really the ultimate goal of any party.

For this dinner, I used my gold sequin tablecloth—a reliable workhorse for a wide range of holiday events. I've paired it with rich burgundies for Rosh Hashanah (the Jewish New Year) and fire engine red linens for Christmas, and, of course, this all gold

Add the finishing touches before guests arrive. Light candles; lay out menus and seating assignments; make sure glass- and flatware are straight and uniformly spaced.

dinner. In the center of the table were gold sculptures (including a Jeff Koons balloon dog), white flowers, and sparkling desserts. Our lollipops with gold leaf doubled as a party favor, but you could also use chocolates in gold wrappers or golden Jordan almonds. To give the table a bit more complexity, I added touches of navy blue, but any jewel tone would work. Candlelight extends the glowy vibe, so load up on tapers and tea lights. There are so many ways to add gold to food—from edible gold leaf (the most expensive option) to gold sprinkles, edible gold spray paint, and a special product called Edible Glitter. If you order any of these gold items online, you can get them more economically. There is lots of creative flexibility with the menu from our ginger cocktail to the tongue-in-cheek 24-Karat Carrot Cake. Put your Midas touch on the gold theme.

When hosting a gilded feast like this one, encourage guests to wear some sparkle. A specific dress code gets guests jazzed and builds anticipation. When gold is the element, there is inherent matchimalism from the decor to the menu to the guests.

ABOVE: We incorporated gold as much as possible. The gold-sequin tablecloth is the star, however; it glitters magically in the candlelight. **OPPOSITE:** Even the carrot cake is embellished with edible gold flakes.

Meringue Caviar Swans

I am constantly racking my brain for appetizers that wow, and this swan does exactly that. The ingredients for the swan itself are inexpensive; it's the time needed to prepare and assemble them that sets them apart. This is not a dish for humid weather, as it'll make the meringue tacky. If you prefer not to use caviar you can substitute with butternut squash purée. This recipe makes meringue for more swans than you'll need, but the extra swans are key because they can replace any that crack when handled. Extra intact swans can be used for decoration.

Makes 16 meringue swans

INGREDIENTS

Egg whites from 4 large pasteurized eggs

1 teaspoon cream of tartar

¼ cup sugar

1.75 ounces caviar

DIRECTIONS

1. Place 1 oven rack in the center of the oven and another just below it. Preheat the oven to 170°F. Line two baking sheets with parchment paper. The swan necks and swan bodies cook for different times, so pipe them onto separate baking sheets.

2. Place the eggs whites, cream of tartar, and sugar in the bowl of a stand mixer with the whisk attachment. Whip at medium speed until stiff peaks form.

3. Once fully whipped, reserve one third of the meringue in a bowl in the refrigerator. This is to attach the swan necks to the swan bodies later. It might need to get rewhipped before assembly.

4. Transfer another one third of the egg whites to a piping bag. Here's an easy way to do this: Put an empty piping bag in a quart container or tall glass and use a rubber spatula to transfer the whipped egg whites to the piping bag. Fill only halfway. Snip the tip of the piping bag, so that the opening is about ⅛ inch wide.

5. On one prepared baking sheet, pipe at least 16 S-shaped "necks," 1 to 1 ¼ inches long, flat onto the parchment-lined baking sheet. Try to make as many as you can.

6. On the other prepared baking sheet, use the remaining one third of whipped egg whites for the swan "bodies." With a spoon, gently dollop a ball that is approximately ½ inch in diameter and ½ inch high. Then flatten the top with the back of a spoon. The circles should not be pancake flat, just balls with flat tops (this will ultimately be the area that the caviar topping sits on). Again, make at least 16, and as many more as you can.

7. Put the bodies on the center rack; the necks on the rack just below. Bake until the meringue is not sticky at all, about 45 minutes for the necks and about 1 hour for the bodies.

8. To assemble: Gently place the swan bodies on a serving platter. Use the reserved meringue as the glue to attach the swan necks to the bodies. Add a dollop of caviar on the flat portion of the body. Serve immediately.

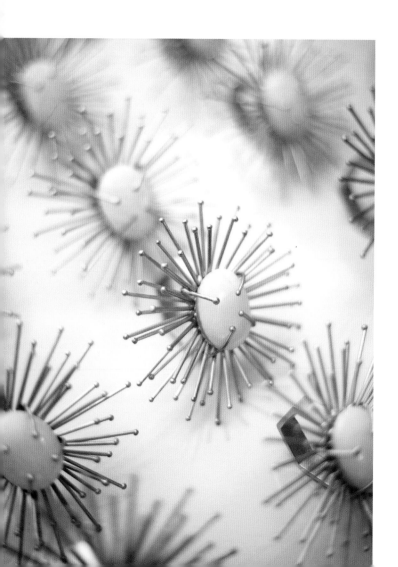

Gingertini

Sure this cocktail is golden amber in color, like champagne and apple juice. And sure, you can have those other drinks on offer, but this unusual flavor fits the profile of the party; it's peppy. This can be batched in advance for simple serving during the party.

Makes 16 drinks

INGREDIENTS

2 cups plus 2 tablespoons freshly squeezed lemon juice

Gold leaf for rim garnish

2 cups ginger liqueur

2 cups bourbon

Ice

DIRECTIONS

1. Before guests arrive, apply the gold leaf to the rim of 16 glasses: In a shallow dish, pour 2 ounces of the lemon juice. Dip the rim of each glass in the lemon juice and then apply the gold leaf to the now wet glass rim so that the gold leaf sticks.

2. In a pitcher, combine the ginger liqueur, bourbon, and remaining lemon juice. Refrigerate until ready to make drinks.

3. When ready, fill a cocktail shaker with ice and add 3 ounces of the cocktail mixture. Shake, then strain into a prepared glass.

ABOVE AND OPPOSITE: I added edible gold leaf to the cocktails and main course (in this case lamb chops).

24-Karat Carrot Cake

In addition to the sweet homophone of the cake name itself, this dessert just really works within the menu. For me, the joy of carrot cake is really the frosting, so lay it on thick!

One (8- or 9-inch two-layer cake); serves 8

INGREDIENTS

CAKE:

1 tablespoon vegetable oil, or an even coating of baking spray, for greasing

4 large egg yolks

1 cup sugar

1 cup olive oil

1 cup all-purpose flour

1 teaspoon ground cinnamon

1 teaspoon ground ginger

½ teaspoon baking powder

½ teaspoon baking soda

½ teaspoon kosher salt

4 to 5 carrots, trimmed, peeled, and grated, or 2 ½ cups store-bought grated carrots

FROSTING:

16 ounces confectioners' sugar

16 ounces cream cheese, at room temperature

3 to 4 tablespoons heavy cream, at room temperature

Edible gold sprinkles or gold leaf flakes for decorating

DIRECTIONS

MAKE THE CAKE:

1. Preheat the oven to 375°F. Grease or spray two 8- or 9-inch round cake pans.

2. In a large bowl, whisk the eggs and sugar until pale yellow, then gradually incorporate the olive oil.

3. In a medium bowl, whisk the flour, cinnamon, ginger, baking powder, baking soda, and salt.

4. Pour the flour mixture into the egg mixture. Use a wooden spoon to mix until the flour is fully incorporated. Add the carrots and combine until evenly distributed.

5. Transfer half the batter to each of the prepared pans with a silicone spatula and smooth the tops.

6. Bake until a knife inserted in the center comes out clean, about 40 minutes.

7. Let rest in the cake pans for 15 minutes before carefully removing and transferring to a cooling rack.

8. Allow the cakes to cool completely before frosting, about 2 hours.

MAKE THE FROSTING:

In a large bowl, use a wooden spoon to combine the confectioners' sugar, cream cheese, and 3 tablespoons of the heavy cream. If the frosting is too thick to spread, add the remaining tablespoon of heavy cream to achieve a desired frosting consistency.

ASSEMBLE THE CAKE:

1. Once the cakes have cooled, place the first layer on your serving platter or cake stand. Use a spatula to layer one third of the frosting in the center. Spread evenly around the top. Place the second layer on top of this.

2. Use another one third of the frosting to cover the outside of the cake to catch all crumbs (this is the crumb coat).

3. Refrigerate for at least 1 hour so the frosting can harden.

4. With the remaining one third of the frosting, frost over the "crumb coat" and top of the cake.

5. Finally, apply gold decoration. If using edible gold leaf, use tweezers. If using gold-colored sprinkles, sprinkle them over the top. Refrigerate until ready to serve.

MENU

Farfalle with meatballs
Ravioli and Pesto
Cacio e Pepe
Sautéed Greens
Rigatoni Cannoli

Pasta Party

Pasta has always been one of my favorite foods, but until I designed pasta-shaped earrings, I had not realized the intense degree to which other people love it too. I enjoy nights dedicated to pasta and inviting friends who share my appreciation for this Italian mainstay. It's a crowd pleaser.

Pasta is an inexpensive food, so this party does not need to break the bank. I kept things economical by foregoing flowers for glass vessels full of dry pasta and fresh herb plants like basil potted in empty tomato cans. Vegetables, including eggplants, peppers, and tomatoes, served as part of the centerpiece to emphasize the color palette and celebrate ingredients that commonly pair with pasta. As an

Real pasta, and resin and pearl pasta accessories, as well as traditional accompaniments, create an original centerpiece—no flowers needed.

ABOVE: Fresh basil can be snipped from this centerpiece for a tasty garnish. **OPPOSITE:** The foundation of the table is a tablecloth inspired by Italian majolica tiles, which further immerses guests in the pasta party theme.

added bonus, these veggies could be eaten after the event—no expensive blooms necessary, and no waste. As a whimsical touch, I put earrings on the vegetables. The tablecloth was inspired by the colors and tiles of Capri and the Amalfi Coast and transported guests from New York to Italy.

At each guest's seat, as a zhuzh, I placed farfalle accessories, so the guests too could coordinate with the theme. It's fun to present a little gift; it puts everyone in a happy mood. In lieu of straws, I used "pastraws," long pasta noodles with a hole large enough to drink through, as they best matched the theme. On the printed menu, I painted all of the pasta shapes featured on the table.

The menu clung closely to the pasta theme from the Vodka Sauce Bloody Mary cocktail to a Rigatoni Cannoli dessert of my own design. Consistency with theme is critical for party success. In between the cocktail and dessert, we had a variety of pasta favorites: cacio e pepe (with brown butter), spaghetti and (mini) meatballs, and a ravioli with pesto. This party definitely gets pasta lovers giddy.

ABOVE: Mini meatball skewers with farfalle and basil and a tomato sauce dip are an adorable twist on the traditional spaghetti and meatballs—and are a perfect one-bite appetizer. **OPPOSITE:** The pasta earrings at each place setting are a fun way for guests to get into the spirit of the party.

Vodka Sauce Bloody Mary

This drink is more than just delicious; it's clever. The "vodka sauce" is of course a play on the iconic pasta dish, and the oregano and red chili flakes play it up.

Makes 8 drinks

INGREDIENTS

4 cups vodka

4 cups tomato juice

5 tablespoons freshly squeezed lemon juice

1 teaspoon dried oregano

2 tablespoons red chili flakes (optional, for rim)

Ice

8 fresh basil leaves, for garnish

DIRECTIONS

1. In a pitcher, combine the vodka, tomato juice, 4 tablespoons of the lemon juice, and the oregano. Refrigerate until ready to serve.

2. If making the chili flake rim, pour the remaining 1 tablespoon lemon juice into a shallow bowl and put the chili flakes on a shallow plate. Dunk the rim of each tumbler into the lemon juice and then into the chili flakes, turning to coat.

3. When ready to serve, add ice to each prepared tumbler, stir the cocktail, and evenly distribute among the glasses. Garnish with a basil leaf.

ABOVE: Yellow peppers are adorned with earrings matching those offered to guests. Miniature cherry tomatoes work as both an element of the decor—a pop of color on the table—and as a delightful nibble for guests before the meal starts.

Homemade Tomato Sauce

If you're going for store-bought, splurge on the best: Carbone or Rao's. Otherwise, make it from scratch. Freeze leftovers in an airtight container for up to 6 months.

Makes 2 cups of sauce

INGREDIENTS

10 large fresh plum tomatoes or one 28-ounce can whole plum tomatoes, chopped

Kosher salt

1 stick (8 tablespoons) unsalted butter, at room temperature

2 tablespoons olive oil

2 small onions, finely chopped

5 garlic cloves, minced

1 tablespoon tomato paste

1 tablespoon sugar

Handful basil leaves

DIRECTIONS

1. Bring a large pot of water to a boil over medium-high heat. If using canned tomatoes, skip to step 5.

2. Use a small paring knife to make two "x" incisions at the top and bottom of each tomato. Prepare a bowl with ice and water and set aside.

3. When the water comes to a boil, add 2 tablespoons salt and the tomatoes. Let the tomatoes boil for 10 to 15 seconds, then transfer to the ice water with a slotted spoon.

4. When the tomatoes are cool enough to handle, gently peel off the skin (it should come off easily). Coarsely chop the tomatoes.

5. Melt the butter at medium heat in small skillet, then raise the heat to medium-high and stir for 3 to 5 minutes until the butter is browned and smells nutty. Set aside.

6. Heat the olive oil in a medium saucepan on medium heat. Add the onions, garlic, and 1 teaspoon salt and cook until the onions are softened and translucent, stirring occasionally, 3 to 4 minutes.

7. Reduce the heat to medium-low and add the tomato paste. Let cook for 1 minute, stirring constantly to ensure it doesn't burn.

8. Add the tomatoes, sugar, basil leaves, and 2 teaspoons salt and stir to combine thoroughly. Increase the heat to high and bring to a boil. Once boiling, reduce the heat to low and simmer, covered, for 30 minutes.

9. Taste and add a generous pinch of salt, if needed. Cook, uncovered, for 30 minutes.

10. Blend with an immersion blender until smooth. Add the brown butter and continue blending until fully incorporated.

11. Transfer about 1 cup of the sauce to a serving bowl and serve alongside the Farfalle-Meatball Bites.

Farfalle-Meatball Bites

At this party, guests were greeted with Farfalle Bites (photo on page 64): mini grape-size meatballs, a basil leaf, and a farfalle bow on a toothpick with homemade tomato sauce for dipping. Mini anything is cute but especially meatballs.

Makes about 24; serves 8

INGREDIENTS

½ pound farfalle, cooked al dente the day of serving, tossed with olive oil, and laid in a single layer on baking sheets

½ pound ground beef (15% fat is my favorite for this)

¼ pound ground veal

1 large egg yolk

1 ½ teaspoons kosher salt

15 fresh basil leaves, halved

½ to 1 cup Homemade Tomato Sauce, for dipping

DIRECTIONS

1. Preheat the oven to 400°F. Line a baking sheet with parchment paper.

2. In a large bowl, combine the beef, veal, yolk, and salt. Roll the meatballs into grape-size balls and place them on the prepared baking sheet. Bake until browned on all sides, about 10 minutes. Let rest until cool enough to handle.

3. On a toothpick, skewer 1 piece farfalle with 1 basil leaf and 1 meatball. Arrange on serving platter with the warm tomato sauce. Serve immediately.

Rigatoni Cannoli

I was determined to create a pasta-derived dessert to surprise and delight. I thought of cannoli, a dessert beloved by my family, best bought on Arthur Avenue in the Bronx or Mulberry Street in Lower Manhattan. It occurred to me that rigatoni's wide tubular shape is similar to cannoli. Bam! Fried rigatoni could become the cannoli tube, filled with sweetened ricotta and cocoa powder.

Makes about 30 cannoli; serves 8

INGREDIENTS

½ pound of rigatoni

Kosher salt

Vegetable oil

2 tablespoons ground cinnamon

2 tablespoons granulated sugar

1 cup whole milk ricotta

2 tablespoons confectioners' sugar

Cocoa powder

DIRECTIONS

1. Cook the rigatoni in a pot of salted boiling water according to the package instructions. Once tender, drain the pasta. Set aside pieces that have broken. Blot the winners dry with paper towels. Roll them in about a tablespoon of oil so that they don't stick together.

2. Heat 1 inch oil in a medium saucepan on medium-high heat until very hot but not smoking. Line a large plate with paper towels. Gradually, add the rigatoni noodles, so as to not overcrowd the pan, and fry until golden and crisp, about 2 minutes. Remove with a slotted spoon and drain on the paper towels. Add more oil to the pan, if needed, and continue frying the remaining pasta.

3. In a shallow bowl or on a small plate, use a fork to combine the cinnamon and granulated sugar.

4. While the rigatoni is still warm, roll in the sugar-cinnamon mixture, shaking off excess. Place on a clean plate and continue to roll the remaining pasta.

5. In a medium bowl, combine the ricotta and confectioners' sugar until incorporated. Transfer the mixture to a piping bag using a rubber spatula. Snip the tip of the piping bag and fill each rigatoni with the ricotta mixture.

6. Set the filled cannoli on a serving platter. Garnish with a dusting of cocoa powder and serve.

THIS PAGE: The display of dry rigatoni next to the cannoli is a visual cue to guests about the unique ingredient starring in the dessert.

Menu

Lychee Martinis
Spring Salad
Cornish Hen
Potato Nests
Chinoiserie Cakes
Blueberry Ice Cream

Blue and White Chinoiserie Dinner

When I saw my friend's dining room in Richmond, Virginia, I was blown away by its classic American beauty. Blue and white on dark wood is my favorite. To me, it's quintessential elegance. It works for all seasons and never goes out of style.

My friend was organizing a dinner of local entrepreneurs and creatives, and she thoughtfully invited me from New York to help put it together. We decided to plan the dinner around the room in which it would be held. The dining room was our North Star: the dark woods, the beautiful moldings, and, of course, the blue-and-white wallpaper. In lieu of a tablecloth, the place mats were the foundation of the tablescape, and we opted for linen in the shape of lotus flowers for their relation to the pattern in

The fantasy for this party was to create a dinner around the beloved color combination of blue and white, inspired by the room's wallpaper. The Chefanie white lotus place mats play off of the foliate details in the pattern.

the wallpaper. The omission of a tablecloth meant the dark wood table could shine, complementing other aspects of the room. White linen on dark wood creates drama. We used my classic blue-and-white transferware plates and my friend's glassware. It was a little mix and match, but it worked. Moreover, we painted white taper candles with blue wax to match the motifs but with inverse colors, so they would pop against the wallpaper. Blue hydrangeas dotted the table in miniature blue and white vases. The blue eyelet dinner napkins worked with the other tableware beautifully, and there was already so much pattern in the room that solid napkins were a good balance.

Food-wise, the Cornish hen on a potato nest directly referenced the wallpaper. This game bird is so old-school and elegant, and the nest is an unusual format for the simple potato. Both can be roasted in the oven, which makes them great dinner party dishes. Guests were wowed when at the end of the meal everyone was presented with a miniature matchimalist cake. I used my decorative cake sheets for these, but you could also decorate individual cakes with white frosting and blue accents, such as blueberries or blue candies.

ABOVE: The North Star was the dining room's blue and white wallpaper, a wonderful example of chinoiserie (the celebration of Chinese motifs in Western formats). The candles were hand-painted in inverse colors to echo the pattern. **OPPOSITE:** This matching skirt and top from Cara Cara allowed me to blend into the party.

OPPOSITE: Mix and match glassware adds a note of informality to this otherwise elegant dark wood table.
ABOVE: Blue hydrangeas were the obvious flower choice in Chefanie bud vases.

Lychee Martini

Lychees are always delicious but especially after stewing in a martini. Plan ahead by sourcing your lychee juice and canned lychees online or at a specialty grocery store.

Makes 16 drinks

INGREDIENTS
3 cups vodka
3 cups lychee juice
32 canned lychees, for garnish
16 toothpicks
Ice
Dry vermouth

DIRECTIONS

1. Before guests arrive, combine the vodka and lychee juice in a pitcher. Refrigerate until ready to serve.

2. Prepare the lychee garnish ahead by spearing two lychees on each toothpick.

3. When ready to serve, fill a cocktail shaker with ice, then add 3 ounces of the vodka-lychee mixture and a splash of vermouth.

4. Shake, then strain into a martini glass. Place a lychee garnish in the glass.

Roasted Cornish Hens with Potato Nest

What I love about Cornish hens are their similarity to chicken but their naturally individual size. These are special occasion birds in my book.

Serves 8

INGREDIENTS
8 russet potatoes, peeled
8 large eggs
3 tablespoons kosher salt
4 teaspoons freshly ground black pepper
8 (1¼-pound) Cornish hens
Handful chives, minced

DIRECTIONS

1. Arrange the oven racks to allow space for the hens and potatoes to roast at the same time. Preheat the oven to 400°F. Line 3 baking sheets with parchment paper.

2. Grate the potatoes into skinny matchsticks using a mandolin or a food processor with the shredding disc. Place the grated potatoes in a kitchen towel and squeeze out the water.

3. Transfer to a large bowl and add the eggs, 1 ½ tablespoons of the salt, and 2 teaspoons of the pepper. Mix with a spoon to thoroughly combine.

4. On 2 of the prepared baking sheets, create 8 disks of the shredded potatoes that are about 7 inches in diameter (make 4 disks on each sheet). Set aside while you prepare the Cornish hens.

5. Use paper towels to pat the Cornish hens dry. Sprinkle the exteriors and cavities with the remaining 1 ½ tablespoons salt and 2 teaspoons pepper. Use kitchen twine to tie the legs together; this will ensure more even cooking. Place them on the remaining baking sheet.

6. Roast the hens and potatoes until the latter are golden brown. The hens are done when the skin is golden, the juices run clear, and an instant-read thermometer registers 160°F. Both should take 50 to 60 minutes.

7. Place a potato "nest" in the center of each plate; place a bird on top; and sprinkle with some of the chives. Plate the remaining servings.

Chinoiserie Cakes

When I started making my patterned cakes with Chefanie sheets, they were referred to as "wallpaper cakes." The ingredients are starches, sugars, and water, mixed together like pancake batter. Then, the batter is spread as thin as paper. We print the designs onto this edible paper. My yellow cake beneath the sheets is a tried-and-true, deliciously simple recipe. Whatever recipe you decide use beneath the sheets, I recommend a white frosting, so the color of the sheets is not changed; a dark chocolate frosting, for example, can ruin the color of the sheets.

Makes 8 (3-inch) cakes; serves 8

INGREDIENTS

CAKES:

Cooking spray

3 cups all-purpose flour

1 ½ teaspoons baking powder

1 ¼ teaspoons baking soda

3 teaspoons kosher salt

1 ½ sticks (12 tablespoons) unsalted butter, at room temperature

1 ½ cups sugar

3 large eggs

1 ½ cups buttermilk

FROSTING:

6 cups confectioners' sugar

1 ½ sticks (12 tablespoons) unsalted butter, at room temperature

½ to ¾ cup heavy cream

Kosher salt

4 to 5 Chefanie Sheets, or 1 to 2 cups blue candies or 1 to 2 cups blueberries (optional)

THIS PAGE: My catering company's uniform happens to be a blue and white apron. I was delighted it worked perfectly with the event decor.
OPPOSITE: Individually portioned chinoiserie cakes tied everything together.

DIRECTIONS

MAKE THE CAKES:

1. Preheat the oven to 350°F. Spray eight 3-inch cake pans with cooking spray.

2. In a medium bowl, whisk the flour, baking powder, baking soda, and ½ teaspoon salt until combined. Set aside.

3. In the bowl of a stand mixer fitted with the paddle attachment, cream the butter and sugar on medium speed until fluffy, about 5 minutes. Beat in the eggs, one at a time, until fully incorporated. On low speed, slowly add the buttermilk until just combined. Add the flour mixture in a couple of additions and beat on low speed until completely smooth. (Alternatively, if working manually, combine the butter and sugar in a large bowl with a fork. Incorporate the eggs, one at a time, using a wooden spoon. Slowly add the buttermilk and stir until just combined. Add the flour mixture in a couple of additions and mix until smooth.)

4. Distribute the batter among the prepared pans, filling them only three-quarters full. Use a silicone spatula to smooth the tops. Bake for 20 to 25 minutes, until a toothpick inserted in the center comes out clean. Allow the cakes to cool for 15 minutes, then remove from the pans and transfer to a cooling rack. Let cool completely.

3. Place each cake on a serving plate. Add enough of a second coat of frosting so that the decoration sticks.

4. If you like, apply patterned Chefanie Sheets (see following instructions), or blue candies or blueberries.

HOW TO DECORATE WITH CHEFANIE SHEETS

1. Using a ruler, measure the height and diameter of your smoothly frosted cake.

2. On the long side of the sheet, cut a line to create a band that is a half an inch taller than the cake's height. Based on the size of your cake, you may need to cut multiple bands. Set aside.

3. To one side of a sheet, measure a square that is ½ inch longer than the cake's diameter. Set aside.

4. To wrap the sides of the cake, remove the band sheets from their backings.

5. On a flat surface (like a cake stand or cutting board), carefully apply the bands to the side of the cake. As there might be slight variation, trim the bands to the exact height of the cake.

6. Once the sides of the cake are wrapped, place the square on top of the cake.

7. Trim the parts of the square that hang off the sides of the cake, transforming the top sheet into a perfect circle.

8. Place the decorated cake in the refrigerator for at least 1 hour or up to 1 day, until you are ready to enjoy.

9. Tag your creations with #ChefanieSheets and you may be featured by @chefanienass!

NOTES

• Buttercream frosting is the ideal frosting; it is wet, but not too wet.

• Use small scissors (like nail or embroidery scissors) to make the most precise cuts.

• For the smoothest slices, cut a cold decorated cake with a very sharp knife.

MAKE THE FROSTING:

While the cakes are cooling, prepare the frosting. Put the sugar, butter, heavy cream, and salt in the bowl of a stand mixer fitted with the paddle attachment. Start mixing on low speed so the sugar doesn't spew out. Gradually increase the speed and cream until smooth, about 2 minutes. (Alternatively, in a large mixing bowl use a fork to combine the sugar, butter, cream, and salt. Mix until smooth.) Taste for salt and add an extra pinch, if needed.

ASSEMBLE THE CAKES:

1. Once the cakes have cooled, transfer them to a cake rack. Cake by cake, spread 1 to 1 ½ tablespoons frosting around the side and top of each cake. This is your crumb coat.

2. Once all cakes are covered with the initial layer of frosting, place on a baking sheet and refrigerate so the frosting hardens, about 1 hour.

Standing Soirées

Standing soirées—unseated gatherings for mingling, generally held between 6 p.m. and 8 p.m.—are a classic party form. Most venues can hold more people standing than they can sitting, and more people are inclined to come if they can stop by. Not to mention that they give you a good bang for your buck: standing parties can accommodate more people more cost effectively than seated dinners.

When people are standing, they cannot cut with fork and knife. Food must be bite-size. Unless specified otherwise, a standing soirée should offer all meal categories—drinks, savories, and sweets—to give guests a taste of whatever they might need in that moment. You can set up as buffet or pass bites. Cheese boards can run the gamut from individual, served in small jars filled with cheese cubes, grapes, and crackers, to expansive (bordering on full-meal buffets).

Hors d'oeuvres, which from French translates to outside the main work, can be the center of attention at a mingling mixer. Budget four hors d'oeuvres per guest per hour, and two to six different types of hors d'oeuvres. The number of hors d'oeuvres you serve depends on how many diets you need to satisfy (vegetarian, gluten-free, etc.) and your budget. They can be homemade, or you can jazz up frozen grocery store hors d'oeuvres by sprinkling on sesame seeds, poppy seeds, Maldon salt, or freshly chopped herbs. You can purchase many kinds of premade accoutrements to fill with dips, chopped meat, or purées. The cones I use in my duck confit cones, for example, are from an online patisserie (see Resources), and they last for six months in my cupboard. You can premake a big batch of soup and portion it into shot glasses and wrap seasonal fruits with prosciutto. The breadth of human creativity can be appreciated by looking through any caterer's menu of passed bites.

Make sure there are places to sit, but scatter seating in small groups to prevent stagnancy.

There are all kinds of ways to zhuzh a standing soirée. At my twenty-first birthday party at the Soho Grand Hotel, guests were invited to wear hats, as this would indicate to the bartender that they were part of the party. These kinds of parties are usually celebratory, so have fun. I believe in statement bites. A friend used to serve rat-shaped chocolates to foster conversation!

Menu

Caprese Cooler

Sicilian Slice
(with assorted toppings)

King Midas Slice

Roasted Broccolini

Rainbow Cookies

Red Gingham Cake

Chic Pizza Party

For my twenty-seventh birthday, I wanted to invite as many friends as possible. Not having a seated dinner meant I could casually introduce friends to one another by signaling across the room, and my only limit on guest count was the space's fire code capacity. Plus, New Yorkers know that pizza is its own sacred food group, so I knew most people would be happy with the food.

As many of my friends are from the fashion set, the party had high standards. My solution was to jazz up a standard dollar-slice pizzeria on Fourteenth Street in Manhattan with live music, patterned cakes, portable pizza slices, and a dress code.

The invitation looked like a pizza box, and set the tone and established the dress code: "Red Saucy Attire." For some that meant an Italian-inspired look; for others that meant a small touch of red. Having a themed dress code ensures that guests think

As a lifelong New Yorker, owning a pizzeria has long been a personal aspiration. For this pop-up party, I created tongue-in-cheek, chicer branding for my fantasy pizza parlor. Everyone received a T-shirt.

about what they wear and how it adds to the event. I wore my signature Chefanie farfalle earrings, the evening's T-shirt, and a whimsical Dolce & Gabbana pasta-printed skirt. I love getting dressed up for a party.

The music inspiration was "live Italian mambo." I composed a set list of songs along these lines and hired an Italian-style accordionist-singer duo. The music created a sense that we were in a version of Little Italy that does not exist anymore. Live music is a zhuzh of party magic that we don't get on a weeknight at home, and it's more conducive to making memories. One of my friends has won *Jeopardy!* several times and knows a lot of song lyrics. He would not have sung along as enthusiastically with a sad cell phone playing music through speakers!

Everyone was given a pizzeria T-shirt—from the cooks to the supermodel guests. Many guests donned it that night, making the night itself fun, and I still see people wearing the shirt around town.

This concept can be easily adapted for a dessert social at an ice cream parlor or a brunch at a bagel bakery. Or, it can be done at home with takeout pizza.

ABOVE AND OPPOSITE: An Italian accordionist sang classics, while the gang noshed on a mostly pizza menu, with some healthier green options on the side.

King Midas Pizza

Whether you rent out your local pizzeria or order pizza to your home, add some zhuzh with gold leaf. However, if you want to make pizza from scratch, try this recipe—a riff on Jim Lahey's famous recipe.

Makes four 10-inch pizzas; serves 8

INGREDIENTS

3 ¾ cups all-purpose flour, plus more for dusting

¼ teaspoon active dry yeast

3 teaspoons kosher salt

1 ½ cups warm water

2 cups Homemade Tomato Sauce (page 68)

1 cup grated mozzarella

8 balls fresh burrata

Edible gold leaf

DIRECTIONS

1. In a large mixing bowl, blend the flour, yeast, and salt with a fork. Add the water and combine thoroughly.

2. Cover the bowl with a damp kitchen towel and then wrap with plastic wrap. Leave in a dry place with no direct sunlight at room temperature for 18 hours, or until it has more than doubled in size.

3. Preheat the oven to 500°F. Line 4 large baking sheets with parchment paper.

4. Dust a work surface with flour and scrape the dough onto it. Divide the dough into 4 equal parts and shape them into flattened 10-inch round pizza pies with your hands.

5. Place each round of dough on a prepared baking sheet. Ladle tomato sauce onto each and spread it around. Distribute the mozzarella cheese evenly among the pizzas.

6. Bake until the crust is golden brown and the cheese is bubbling, 5 to 8 minutes. You may need to cook the pizzas in batches if you can't fit all four baking sheets in the oven at once.

7. When the pizzas come out of the oven, distribute dollops of burrata on each pizza (2 balls per pie) and use tweezers to decorate with the edible gold leaf. Slice into 8 slices per pie. Serve immediately.

Caprese Cocktail

Love a cocktail that doubles as a snack! The longer the skewer of caprese garnish, the better. This drink can be batched ahead of serving.

Makes 8 drinks

INGREDIENTS

24 cherry tomatoes

16 to 24 bocconcini (mini mozzarella balls)

16 to 24 fresh basil leaves

1 ½ cups vodka, chilled

½ cup balsamic vinegar, chilled

DIRECTIONS

1. Use extra-long toothpicks to skewer alternating tomatoes, mozzarella, and basil.

2. In a large pitcher, stir together the vodka and balsamic vinegar. Refrigerate until ready to serve, up to 12 hours in advance.

3. For each cocktail, restir, pour into a cocktail glass, and add a tomato-mozzarella garnish.

OPPOSITE AND ABOVE: Desserts were inspired by true Italian-American classics like rainbow cookies. The giant tiered cake has a patterned decoration that evokes the red and white checkered tablecloths found at casual Italian-American eateries.

Rainbow Cookies

The combination of almond, raspberry, and chocolate in these cookies is personally so nostalgic. They are always delicious, but when made at home, they are even better—softer and richer. You can mix up the colors for different occasions.

Makes 24 cookies

INGREDIENTS

4 large eggs, separated

3 sticks (24 tablespoons) unsalted butter, softened

1 cup sugar

8 ounces almond paste

¼ cup whole milk

1 teaspoon almond extract

2 cups all-purpose flour

2 or 3 food colorings of your choice (I used red and dark green; one layer didn't have color)

1 cup raspberry jam

1½ cups semisweet chocolate chips

1 teaspoon vegetable oil

DIRECTIONS

1. Preheat the oven to 325°F. Line three 9 x 13-inch baking pans with parchment paper.

2. In a stand mixer with the whisk attachment, whisk the egg whites to stiff, fluffy peaks, about 5 minutes. Transfer to a bowl and set aside.

3. Clean the bowl of the stand mixer and attach the paddle. Add the butter, sugar, and almond paste. Mix on medium speed until smooth, about 5 minutes, making sure to scrape the sides of the mixer occasionally. Once smooth, add the 4 egg yolks, milk, and almond extract and mix on medium speed until evenly incorporated, about 3 minutes. Add the flour gradually and mix on low speed until evenly combined.

4. Use a rubber spatula to carefully fold the egg whites into this mixture, being careful not to deflate them.

5. Put one third of the mixture into a medium bowl and do the same with another third. To these bowls, add 1 or 2 drops of desired food coloring and fold in. You may need to add another drop or two to make the desired color.

6. Transfer each color into a different prepared baking pan, making sure that the batter is a consistent thickness. Use a rubber spatula or a knife to spread the batter evenly. You can use a toothpick to check that the height of the batter is the same in each pan.

7. Bake until the cakes bounce back lightly when touched and a toothpick inserted in the center of each cake comes out clean, 10 to 12 minutes.

8. Allow the cakes to cool in their pans at room temperature for 1 hour.

9. Put the bottom layer of cake on a baking sheet, parchment paper side up. Peel off the parchment paper. Spread half of the jam on this bottom layer. Using a wide spatula, gently place the second layer of cake on top of the first layer, parchment paper side up. Peel off the parchment paper. Spread the other half of the jam over the second layer. Top with the last cake layer, parchment paper side up. Peel off the parchment paper.

10. After the three layers of cake have been assembled, cover in plastic wrap and allow to chill in the refrigerator for at least 1 hour and up to 2 days.

11. Put the chocolate in a microwave-safe bowl and microwave to melt, stirring at 30-second increments. Once melted, mix in the oil and spread the chocolate mixture over the top of the cake.

12. Allow the chocolate to set in a cool room away from sunlight, about 2 to 3 hours. The chocolate should not be dripping but it should not harden completely, otherwise it will crack when you cut the cake into cookie-size rectangles.

13. Using a slicing knife, trim off the edges of the cake, then cut the cake into 1 x 2-inch rectangles. For sharp, clean lines, wipe the knife in between each cut.

14. Arrange on a platter and serve.

Menu

Classic Martini

Dirty Martini

Espresso Martini

Lychee Martini

Schoolnight Mocktini

Martini Party

Though always chic, martinis have inspired a lot of excitement recently. When held in its standard V-shaped glass, a martini forces its drinker to adopt a posture that turns any night into a special occasion. I wanted to create a celebration of this festive cocktail. My inspiration was the sexy late-night vibe of the Nines, an old-school piano lounge in downtown Manhattan. The menu was a celebration of the martini with five variations. Four were familiar, but the fifth (School-Night Mocktini) allowed the nondrinkers to have something to sip.

I complemented the cocktails with creative snacks. I purchased a giant sixty-pound wheel of Pecorino Romano for standing Cacio e Pepe. Pasta made with cheese and pepper, cacio e pepe is one of my favorite pasta dishes because of its

There are so many varieties of martinis, and I wanted to celebrate this timeless cocktail with a dedicated party. The menu featured four classic martinis as well as one virgin option: the School-Night Mocktini.

delicious simplicity. Moreover, the wheel itself became a party prop, as the pasta was prepared in front of guests. Chicken tenders with honey mustard circulated on silver trays. The sweet bites, on the other hand, were inspired by my love of surrealism. The "finger" cookies were my signature shortbread recipe and did not even require any special equipment like a cookie cutter. The "nails" were almonds, and I created the indentations of knuckles with a bamboo skewer. Pretzel rods, a familiar bar snack, became "cigarettes" with melted white chocolate and Oreo "ashes." A signature Chefanie treat, our "cocktail almonds" are chocolate-covered and look like cocktail olives.

When choosing my look, I thought of Cher and her long hair, as well as '70s nightclubs. I straightened my hair and wore gold head-to-toe. There were zhuzhes everywhere: cocktail napkins in the shape of cocktail olives or with embroidery inspired by my drawings, which elevated the presentation of the foods served. I hired a piano-playing singer, who covered sultry classics like "Spooky" by Dusty Springfield. He dressed up in a black velvet cape and helped to set a theatrical mood.

ABOVE AND OPPOSITE: At the Salmagundi Club in Manhattan, I hosted one hundred friends for a night of martinis and live music. I wanted to recreate a piano bar's sultriness, so I hired a pianist to play (and sing) '70s ballads. It was fun to dress up in cocktail party attire.

1. Before guests arrive and to batch prepare this recipe, combine the vodka, cold brew concentrate, coffee liqueur, syrup, and vanilla. Refrigerate up to 12 hours in advance.

2. When making each drink to serve, fill a cocktail shaker with ice, stir the mixture, and add 2½ ounces to the shaker.

3. Shake for 20 to 30 seconds so that the natural oils from the ingredients combine with air bubbles and form foam. Strain into a martini glass.

4. Garnish with coffee beans, simply sprinkled on top.

School-Night Mocktini

This recipe was designed for my pregnant and nondrinking friends who would not partake in alcohol at my party. In the current sober-curious environment, there are many varieties of virgin spirits. The recipe includes my favorite for this recipe, purchased online ahead of the event.

Makes 8 drinks

INGREDIENTS

2 cups Damrak Virgin 0.0, or another nonalcoholic gin

½ cup olive brine

Ice

8 to 16 olives for garnish

DIRECTIONS

1. Combine the nonalcoholic gin and olive brine. Refrigerate for up to 12 hours.

2. When making each drink to serve, fill a cocktail shaker with ice and add 2 ½ ounces of the cocktail mixture. Shake, then strain into a martini glass. Garnish with olives.

Homemade Espresso Martini

Bartenders are generally well equipped to make perfect, artisanal espresso martinis with fresh foam. At a party, when you want to pre-batch and prepare as much as possible in advance, it's a different story. Use cold brew concentrate if you are batching this or freshly pulled espresso if you are making everything à la minute.

Makes 16 drinks

INGREDIENTS

2 cups plus 2 tablespoons vodka or coffee-infused vodka

1 cup plus 2 tablespoons fresh espresso or cold brew concentrate

1 cup coffee liqueur

½ cup plus 2 tablespoons Demerara syrup

2 tablespoons vanilla extract

Ice

16 coffee beans for garnish

Pretzel Cigarettes

In a nod to a former time when cigarettes accompanied martinis, I wanted to create the closest thing: a trompe l'oeil cigarette made with pantry ingredients. Guests appreciated the humor and, ultimately, the toothsome confection.

Serves 8

INGREDIENTS

4 Oreo cookies, white filling discarded and cookies blitzed in a food processor until dusty

1 tablespoon sugar

16 (4-inch-long) pretzel rods

1 (12-ounce) bag white chocolate chips

DIRECTIONS

1. Line a baking sheet with parchment or wax paper.

2. Mix the Oreo dust with the granulated sugar in a small bowl. This will be used for the "ashes."

3. Put the chocolate chips in a tall microwave-safe drinking glass and melt in 30-second increments on normal power, stirring well after each increment, until fully melted.

4. Dip the rod into the melted chocolate three quarters of the way up the pretzel. Shake off any excess chocolate so that the chocolate generally maintains the shape of the pretzel.

5. Dip the tip of the chocolate-coated pretzel into the "ashes."

6. Lay each coated pretzel on the prepared baking sheet and allow to cool. Once cool, arrange the rods on a serving platter or in a jar. If you like, put any remaining Oreo "ashes" in a small dish to be the "ashtray" and place beside the "cigarettes."

Cacio e Pepe

I love dishes that are theatrical and incorporate their preparation into how they are presented. Preparing this pasta dish in a giant wheel of cheese in front of guests is a wow. You can source the wheel online, from a food distributor, or (with enough advance notice) potentially from your local grocer. After the event, you can grate and freeze the cheese for future use.

Serves 8

INGREDIENTS

60-pound wheel Pecorino Romano, hollowed out at the top to form a bowl shape (approximately 2 to 4 inches deep; use pieces removed to grate)

3 pounds spaghetti, cooked until almost al dente and tossed in olive oil

Salt

2 cups freshly grated Pecorino Romano

Black pepper

DIRECTIONS

1. Move your cheese wheel so it is beside your pasta pot and visible to guests.

2. In a pot of boiling salted water, reheat individual servings of cooked pasta for 1 to 2 minutes. As the pot boils down and water runs lower, you can add additional water (and salt).

3. Using tongs, transfer the reheated pasta to the well of the cheese wheel. Add ½ cup pasta water and a sprinkle of the grated cheese. Toss the pasta around the well until it is coated with a slippery cheese sauce.

4. Transfer the pasta to a plate and freshly crack black pepper over the top. Serve immediately. Continue this process until all guests are served.

Menu
Honeycrisp Cocktail
Tomato Soup
Corn Soup
Squash Soup
Onion Soup
Garnishes!
Honey Pie
Hand Pies

Fall Soup Party

Fall is the kickoff of the festive season, and it's also when (what feels like) everyone is in New York. The city is at its best, and it's a great time of year to have people over. I have always wanted to host a soup-driven party. Soup is ideal for a standing soirée; like cocktails, it can be sipped from individual vessels, with or without a spoon. Moreover, soup is a comforting, nourishing food—and each one is so distinct. Additionally, if you serve a variety, you can be inclusive of most diets: gluten-free, nut-free, vegan, etc. For example, you can serve an onion soup made with beef stock and served with bread and cheese, but you can also do a meat-, dairy-, and gluten-free tomato, corn, or squash soup. Importantly, since the event is not seated, people can swing by when they can and stay as long as they like—and you can host a bigger group. Since most soups can almost entirely be made in advance, day-of preparation is a lot less stressful.

In the fall, temperatures drop and there's a bounty of end-of-summer and fall produce to enjoy. A soup party is a fun concept—one in which guests can really tailor their own consumption. For some, it can be as filling as a meal at a seated event; for others, it can be a lighter appetizer-like meal.

HONEY PIE

MAPLE PECAN

SQUASH SEEDS

GARNISHES

CORN SOUP

ONION SOUP

SQUASH SOUP

TOMATO SOUP

There are many ingredients available in the fall, benefiting from the final kick of summer produce (corn, tomatoes) as well as its own signature veggies. For this party, I took advantage of all of these ingredients, which also happen to be colorful. If you're building a party around a single type of food, I think you need at least three options; for this one, I made four soups. Some can be served out of a pot with a ladle; you can keep these simmering on the stove over a very low heat so they stay warm for the duration of the event. Soups can also be served in carved out pumpkins or squashes, drinking glasses, teacups, or whatever other vessels you might have at hand. If serving soups in alternative vessels, refresh often so guests get warm soup— or encourage guests to take from a pot that is simmering. You can lay out garnishes, napkins, and spoons on a kitchen island or dining table. My garnish station had candied and roasted nuts, crackers, cheese sticks, and bite-size grilled cheeses. For visual variety in the display, we made bread sculptures and served the cocktail in a tall pitcher. The sweet options were honey pie and mixed hand pies.

This is a fun party concept that also feeds people a substantial amount of food.

ABOVE AND OPPOSITE: We set up this soup party so that guests could help themselves to any variety of soups and/or garnishes. You can save seeds from hollowed-out squashes and roast them—they are delicious—and there's no easier no-fuss nibble than pecans.

Candied Pecans

In addition to being a great nibble on your soup garnish bar, these also make delicious bar snacks and treats on cheese boards.

Makes 2 cups

INGREDIENTS

2 cups pecan halves

2 large egg whites

2 tablespoons sugar

2 tablespoons maple syrup

1 teaspoon ground cinnamon

1 teaspoon kosher salt

DIRECTIONS

1. Arrange a rack in the center of the oven and preheat to 350°F. Line a baking sheet with parchment paper.

2. In a small bowl, stir together the nuts, egg whites, sugar, maple syrup, cinnamon, and salt.

3. Arrange the coated pecans on the prepared baking sheet. Bake on the center rack until the nuts are crystallized and dry, 30 to 40 minutes, stirring every 10 minutes.

4. Let cool completely, then transfer to an airtight container and store for up to 1 week.

Honeycrisp Cocktail

This drink requires no shaking or stirring for each drink. You can batch the whole thing a few hours in advance of guests' arrival. Easy!

Makes 8 drinks

INGREDIENTS

2 cups white rum

3 Honeycrisp apples, cut into thin matchsticks and tossed in lemon juice

1 teaspoon sugar

1 teaspoon cinnamon

DIRECTIONS

Combine all ingredients in a pitcher. Refrigerate until ready to serve. Make sure that each drink includes some of the apple matchsticks.

Squash Soup

Acorn squashes make such adorable natural bowls, and the colors are so autumnal. For the soup itself, you can add other kinds of roasted squash, including butternut. You can also substitute the water with vegetable or chicken stock.

Serves 8

INGREDIENTS

14 acorn squashes

3 tablespoons olive oil

5 teaspoons kosher salt, plus more as needed

1 medium yellow onion, diced

2 teaspoons ground cinnamon

DIRECTIONS

1. Put a rack in the center of the oven and preheat to 425°F.

2. Cut off the stem and the bottom of 6 of the squashes. Slice them into 8 wedges.

Remove the seeds and discard.

3. Scoop out the flesh of the squash and discard the skin. Place the flesh pieces on a baking sheet.

4. For the remaining 8 squashes, cut 1 inch off the top of each squash; set these tops with stems aside. Cut the bottom of the squash so that it can stand flat.

5. Scoop out the seeds and discard. Cut some flesh from the squash, leaving a ½-inch thickness of flesh all around. Place the flesh on the baking sheet with the rest of the squash flesh. Set aside the squash bowls until ready to serve.

6. Toss the squash flesh with 2 tablespoons oil and 3 teaspoons salt.

Roast on the center rack until tender and just starting to brown, 25 to 35 minutes.

7. Heat the remaining 1 tablespoon oil in a large pot and add the onion. Add 1 teaspoon salt. Cook, stirring occasionally, until the onions just start to brown, 5 to 10 minutes.

8. Add the cinnamon, stir, and cook until fragrant, about 1 minute. Add the roasted squash and just enough water to cover, about 8 cups. Bring to a boil. Reduce the heat and simmer until the squash is completely tender, about 20 minutes.

9. Use an immersion blender to puree the soup until smooth. Taste and add the remaining 1 teaspoon salt, if needed. Ladle the warm soup into the squash bowls and serve.

SQUASH SOUP

Onion Soup

This French bistro classic is adapted to a family-style format, including floating slices of bread with melted Gruyère. If the pot of soup is sitting out too long, the bread will disintegrate, so prepare extra cheesy bread to sub in. I use water in this recipe, but you can substitute the more traditional beef stock, which makes a very rich broth.

Serves 8

INGREDIENTS

3 tablespoons olive oil

15 yellow onions, thinly sliced

2 tablespoons kosher salt

2 tablespoons sugar, plus more as needed

3 cloves garlic, minced

1 teaspoon freshly ground black pepper

1 tablespoon fresh thyme leaves

1 baguette, sliced into ¼-inch-thick rounds

12 ounces Gruyère, thinly sliced to match the size of the bread

DIRECTIONS

1. Warm the oil in a large pot over medium-high heat. Place the onions in the pot with the salt and sugar. Cook, stirring frequently, until the onions are deeply browned and caramelized, 30 to 40 minutes.

2. Add the garlic and pepper, and stir to incorporate. As the skillet begins to brown on the bottom, add ¼ cup water to deglaze the pan, scraping bits off the bottom and bringing to a simmer.

3. Add just enough water so that onions are submerged in the liquid, about 8 cups.

Bring to a boil over high heat. Reduce the heat and simmer until the onions are totally soft and the liquid is brown, about 20 minutes. Taste and season with salt, if needed.

4. While the soup simmers, make the cheesy toasts. Preheat the oven to 400°F.

Arrange the bread slices on a parchment-lined baking sheet and top each with a slice of cheese. Bake until the cheese melts, 6 to 10 minutes.

5. To serve, place several of the cheesy toasts in the pot of warm onion soup. Ladle the soup and a toast into individual bowls.

Tomato Soup

In the category of tomato soup, there are so many directions in which to go. This soup is hearty but definitely not heavy, a take on the classic combination of tomato soup and grilled cheese. For eight servings of soup, I made four grilled cheese sandwiches that were cut into 1-inch squares.

Serves 8

INGREDIENTS

2 tablespoons olive oil

3 pounds ripe Roma tomatoes, roughly chopped

1 yellow onion, roughly chopped

3 cloves garlic, minced

2 teaspoons kosher salt, plus more as needed

½ teaspoon freshly ground black pepper, plus more as needed

2 teaspoons sugar

1 tablespoon heavy cream (optional)

DIRECTIONS

1. Heat the olive oil in a large pot over medium heat. Add the tomatoes, onion, garlic, salt, and pepper. Cook, stirring occasionally, until the tomatoes begin to soften and break down, 10 to 15 minutes.

2. Use an immersion blender to puree until smooth. Stir in the sugar and taste for salt and pepper, adding more if needed. Add cream for extra richness, if desired.

3. Ladle the soup into individual serving bowls with a couple squares of grilled cheese.

Corn Soup

This soup is all about the corn, so buy the freshest available (preferably from a farmers' market). It can be served chilled or warm, depending on the weather.

Serves 8

INGREDIENTS

15 ears corn, shucked

2 tablespoons olive oil

1 medium yellow onion, diced

3 teaspoons kosher salt, plus more as needed

DIRECTIONS

1. Remove the kernels from the cobs in a large bowl; keep the kernels and cobs separate.

2. Heat 1 tablespoon of the oil in a large pot, then add the onion and corn kernels. Season with 1 ½ teaspoons salt. Sauté, stirring occasionally, until the onion and corn kernels are just starting to brown, about 10 minutes.

3. Add 15 cups of water, the corn cobs, and 1 ½ teaspoons salt. Bring to a boil, then reduce the heat to low and simmer until the cobs are tender to the touch, about 30 minutes.

4. Remove the cobs from the pot and discard. Purée the soup with an immersion blender until smooth. Taste and season with salt, if needed.

5. Serve immediately or, if serving chilled, allow to cool down for 1 to 2 hours, then chill in the refrigerator for at least 10 hours and up to 24 hours.

TOMATO SOUP

Honey Pie

This is an all-American take on a classic honey dessert. You can make the pie crust from scratch or use store-bought. It's a lovely recipe for Rosh Hashanah, Thanksgiving, or any time you want a simple sweet.

Serves 8

CRUST

2 ½ cups unbleached all-purpose flour, plus more for dusting

2 teaspoons sugar

1 teaspoon kosher salt

2 sticks (16 tablespoons) unsalted butter, cut into small pieces and frozen, plus more for pan

¼ cup ice water

FILLING

1 ¾ cups honey

6 tablespoons (¾ stick) unsalted butter

8 large eggs

1 teaspoon vanilla extract

1 teaspoon freshly grated nutmeg

2 teaspoons kosher salt

DIRECTIONS

FOR THE CRUST (if making from scratch):

1. Place the flour, sugar, and salt in a food processor and mix until combined. Add the butter and pulse until the mixture resembles coarse meal, about 10 seconds. Drizzle the ice water evenly over the mixture. Pulse until the dough just begins to come together (it should not be wet or sticky). If the dough is too dry, add more ice water, 1 tablespoon at a time, and pulse.

2. Shape the dough into a large disk and wrap in plastic wrap. Refrigerate until firm, at least 1 hour.

FOR THE FILLING:

1. Warm the honey in a medium saucepan over low heat until it loosens and becomes more liquid. Remove the pan from the heat and stir in the butter until melted. Set aside for 3 to 5 minutes.

2. In a medium bowl, whisk the eggs, vanilla, nutmeg, and salt. Slowly pour the honey mixture into the bowl and mix until incorporated. Cover and refrigerate until cooled, up to 1 hour.

ASSEMBLE THE PIE:

1. Grease a 9-inch pie plate. On a lightly floured surface, roll out the dough to a ¼-inch thickness. Drape the dough into the prepared pie plate. Trim the overhang. Prick the bottom of the dough with a fork. Refrigerate 30 to 60 minutes.

2. Arrange one oven rack in the center and one rack in the bottom third of the oven. Preheat the oven to 350°F.

3. Blind bake the crust: Line the crust with parchment paper and fill with dried beans or pie weights. Bake the crust on the center rack for 15 minutes. Remove the parchment with beans or pie weights and bake until the crust is golden brown, about 10 minutes more. Cool on a wire rack for at least 20 minutes.

4. Stir the cooled filling and pour it into the cooled crust. Bake on the bottom rack until the center is set, 30 to 35 minutes.

LEFT: Hand pies are another fun treat for a fall gathering. Filling options are endless: savory (chicken pot pie, meatball parm, creamed spinach) and sweet (caramelized apples, Nutella, poppy seeds). I make them by rolling out pie crust and then cutting with festive cookie cutters. The exact timing and ideal temperature depends on the size and thickness of your hand pies, but bake at 375°F until golden brown.

MENU
🍹 Watermelon Margaritas
Guacamole
🥑 Emerald Chicken Salad
Veggie Burgers
🍉 Bouquet of Fruit
Key Lime Pie Popsicles

LOBSTER BAKE
Caprese Salad
Lobster
Sirloin Steak
Mac and Cheese
Corn on the Cob
Roasted Vegetables
Chocolate Meringue Cake

Outdoor Dining

I relish eating al fresco. Outdoor dining can mean your backyard, a local park, a field of sunflowers, or a Christmas tree farm. It can be a picnic in a forest or park, or a candlelit dinner by a river. Much of the time, outdoor venues are affordable or even free, and you don't even need to pay for much decor—the ambiance is already there.

Weather is always a factor in outdoor dining. It's standard to check the weather forecast for the expected temperature and precipitation. In addition to these factors, check the anticipated wind levels. Make sure guests are equipped with shawls, blankets, hats, or umbrellas, if needed. You can provide these items or advise guests to bring their own in advance of the gathering. Candles lit outdoors should have hurricanes to protect them from breezes, and don't use flowers that are top-heavy, as they are more likely to topple over. The best flowers for outdoor dining are low and robust: this can mean arrangements in water-heavy bud vases or long floral runners, fixed in place using fully watered Oasis floral foam. In the days preceding the event, check the time of the sunset and the moon phase. If you have the chance, watch the paths of the sun and the moon relative to your dining area. Use this information to shield guests from uncomfortable sunrays with umbrellas or by putting tables beneath tree branches; alternatively, if it's going to be a moonless night, be sure to provide additional illumination in the form of twinkle lights, candles, or tiki torches.

In order to transport the food to and from your setting, make sure you have enough trays and baskets. Have a plan for collecting dirty dishes, cups, utensils, and linens, like cardboard boxes or large plastic bins. And be sure to provide insect repellent, suntan lotion, and sanitizing wipes. Depending on the duration and location, strongly consider tents and restroom options.

MENU

Watermelon Margaritas

Guacamole

Emerald Chicken Salad

Veggie Burgers

Bouquet of Fruit

Key Lime Pie Popsicles

Pool Party

A pool party can mean a swimming party, but it doesn't have to. On a hot day, just being by the pool under a tree's shade feels cooler than other outdoor alternatives, so it's a lovely place to gather. A pool is a venue that is conducive to many kinds of fun—from chatting to drinking frozen margaritas and swimming, if guests would like.

I love a pool party because it's generally near enough to a house that you have access to amenities like a bathroom or refrigerator, so the stakes of forgetting something are lower than other outdoor alternatives. Moreover, pool parties are so casual that people can come and go as they please. You can tell guests to bring a swimsuit, but it's nice to provide towels and any other swimming accoutrements.

The ideal menu for a hot day by the pool includes light and cool foods. Salads are great, just be sure to choose sturdy lettuces like kale and spinach, which keep

Inspired by the colors of my parents' garden, I designed a table to match, using a Chefanie block-printed mixed poppy tablecloth. The menu items were refreshing and cooling; at the peak of summer, no one wants hot, heavy food.

their crunchy snap longer than delicate greens like mâche and butter lettuce. Chicken paillard complements a green salad and is nice served cold or at room temperature. Fruit skewers are easy to prepare and can be presented on a large pineapple or on a simple tray. You can also place fresh fruit in bowls for guests to serve themselves. Make innovative popsicles with any kind of purée of fruit or juice. You can adapt favorite pies to a popsicle format by freezing the basic pie components in a popsicle mold. Use compotes or juice concentrates, sweetened condensed milk, and something crunchy to represent the crust, like graham cracker or shortbread crumbles. Citrus flavors are especially refreshing on a hot day, which is what inspired my Key Lime Pie Popsicles. Another nice thing about popsicles? They're pretty much one step, unless you do something ambitious like dipping or drizzling them with melted chocolate.

For drinks, have plenty of water on hand and include a frozen cocktail. You can blend frozen fruits, like mango, strawberries, or watermelon, with your favorite spirit.

Take your color-palette inspiration from the surrounding flora.

OPPOSITE AND ABOVE: I kept the palette for my attire—and the table— summery with pinks and blues.

ABOVE: A pineapple holds fruit skewers—a creative and pretty way to present this refreshing snack.
OPPOSITE: A woven decorative tray is an essential tool in your summertime decorating arsenal.

Emerald Kale Salad

Inspired by my favorite salad at the Palm Beach Grill, this recipe is adapted for a pool party anywhere you are. The ingredient list for the dressing is a bit long, but the alchemy of all the flavors makes it totally worthwhile, plus you'll likely have leftover dressing that can be enjoyed for several days.

Serves 8

INGREDIENTS

DRESSING

¾ cup peanut oil

¼ cup rice vinegar

2 tablespoons soy sauce

1 tablespoon freshly squeezed lemon juice

2 teaspoons honey

1 ½ teaspoons Dijon mustard

1 teaspoon sesame oil

1 teaspoon Worcestershire sauce

½ teaspoon freshly ground black pepper

1 garlic clove, minced

SALAD

2 bunches lacinato kale, stemmed and thinly sliced

¾ cup unsalted roasted peanuts, roughly chopped

5 ounces Pecorino Romano, grated (about ¼ cup)

1 rotisserie chicken, skinned and shredded

DIRECTIONS

Make the dressing: In a large measuring cup, combine the peanut oil, rice vinegar, soy sauce, lemon juice, honey, Dijon mustard, sesame oil, Worcestershire sauce, pepper, and garlic and whisk to thoroughly incorporate.

MAKE THE SALAD:

1. In a large serving bowl and with clean hands, massage the kale for about 3 minutes until the leaves soften.

2. Add the peanuts, Pecorino Romano, and chicken and toss together. Pour ¼ cup of the dressing on the salad and toss. If the salad seems too dry, add another ¼ cup. Leftover dressing can be refrigerated in an airtight container for up to 1 week.

3. Place the salad in a serving bowl, if passing at the table, or on individual salad plates. Serve immediately.

Each colorful place setting emphasizes the vibrancy of summer.

1. Put the watermelon chunks in a blender with the ice, lime juice, tequila, and triple sec. Blend on high speed until all of the ingredients are smooth and combined.

2. Divide among 8 cups and serve immediately with either or both optional garnishes.

Key Lime Pie Popsicles

The tart sweetness of key lime pie is so refreshing on a hot day. I adapted this flavor profile to a frozen treat to make it even better.

Makes 10 popsicles

INGREDIENTS

2 cups key lime juice (store-bought is fine)

2 (14-ounce) cans sweetened condensed milk

8 graham crackers, crumbled

DIRECTIONS

1. Use a fork to mix the key lime juice and condensed milk in a large measuring cup.

2. Carefully pour the liquid mixture into popsicle molds, filling each cavity three quarters of the way full. Place the molds in the freezer. After 1 hour, insert popsicle sticks. Freeze for at least 12 hours total or up to 1 month.

3. When ready to serve, unmold the popsicles and press each side into the graham cracker crumbles, coating all sides completely.

Watermelon Margarita

For this cocktail a good blender makes all the difference. What's key here for any pool party cocktail is using a reusable vessel that is not glass, like melamine; nothing ruins a barefoot party like broken glass. You can garnish with watermelon cubes or mint leaves, or both.

Makes 8 drinks

INGREDIENTS

½ large watermelon, seeded and flesh cut into chunks

1 cup ice

2 tablespoons freshly squeezed lime juice

8 ounces tequila

4 ounces triple sec

Small watermelon cubes (optional garnish)

Mint leaves (optional garnish)

ABOVE: A frozen watermelon margarita is summer in a glass and the beverage of choice at a poolside party.
OPPOSITE: Popsicles are easy to make and a great treat to have on hand in your freezer, not to mention being a total delight on a hot day.

MENU

Caprese Salad
Lobster
Sirloin Steak
Mac and Cheese
Corn on the Cob
Roasted Vegetables
Chocolate Meringue Cake

Lobster Bake

What is better than a summer day by the breezy shore? Not much, except finishing it with a traditional lobster bake. This meal around giant crustaceans is not an everyday meal, but it is one of my best loved each summer, as it includes so many of my favorite foods. This special meal brings me to my summer happy place. Preparing a lobster bake for a party of handpicked friends is even better.

The Inn at Perry Cabin, in St. Michael's, Maryland, invited me to their historic property, and I knew that I wanted to do an all-American Lobster Bake on the banks of the Miles River in their backyard. The area is known for seafood, and the iconic setting was appropriate for this classic meal. As much as possible, I wanted to include local elements, although we used lobster instead of crab. Maryland loves its Old Bay Seasoning, so I included it as the rim of the signature cocktail, for example.

We celebrated shellfish with a lobster bake on the Chesapeake Bay;
the decor was red and white.

Although lobster has a luxurious reputation, none of the items on the menu are fastidious. My lobsters are simply boiled in salty water and then baked to extract any excess liquid. Caprese salad comes together in a jiffy with only some arrangement required. Corn on the cob is kissed with a little heat and seasoning, not much else. The Meringue Chocolate Cake is a little topsy-turvy and imperfect, but nonetheless delicious.

The menu, with its reds (tomatoes, lobsters), yellows (corn, macaroni & cheese, lemons), and browns (steak, chocolate cake), inspired the color palette for everything else. The table linens were a mix of red and white. My red and white toile was a nod to the traditional red and white gingham so often associated with a lobster bake, but more elegant. I also kept in mind that guests would be wearing the disposable lobster bibs that are so kitschy and sweet, so I continued the red and white theme to the glassware and candles. The flowers were what was available in my desired colors at the local Maryland grocery store. I wore white with bamboo accessories to tie in with the rest of the elements.

ABOVE AND OPPOSITE: Red and white flowers in bud vases and candles in interesting shapes, as well as brown wood elements, elevate what is usually a very casual tablescape to something a bit more elegant.

LOBSTER BAKE

Caprese Salad
Lobster
Sirloin Steak
Mac and Cheese
Corn on the Cob
Roasted Vegetables
Chocolate Meringue Cake

Mac & Cheese

As someone with an endless appetite for macaroni & cheese—and who has tried many iterations of it all over the United States—this is my favorite version. It's gooey with an English mustard kick.

Serves 8 to 10

INGREDIENTS

9 tablespoons (1 stick plus 1 tablespoon) unsalted butter

2 pounds rigatoni or other tubular pasta

Kosher salt

2 tablespoons olive oil

½ cup all-purpose flour

2 cups whole milk

2 cups heavy cream

2 ¼ cups plus 1 tablespoon grated Pecorino Romano

2 ¼ cups plus 1 tablespoon grated Gruyère

1 tablespoon dry English mustard, such as Colman's

2 tablespoons panko

DIRECTIONS

1. Preheat the oven to 375°F. Butter a 9 x 13-inch baking dish with 1 tablespoon of the butter.

2. Bring a large pot of salted water to a boil. Once boiling, add your pasta and cook to al dente according to the directions on the pasta box.

3. Drain the pasta in a colander and transfer to a large bowl. Coat with the olive oil to prevent the pasta from sticking together. Set aside.

4. In a medium saucepan over medium heat, melt the remaining 8 tablespoons butter, moving it around with a wooden spoon. Add the flour, stirring constantly, until the mixture (a roux), thickens and colors to a golden paste. Reduce the heat to medium-low and slowly add the milk and heavy cream, stirring constantly. Continue to stir until the sauce thickens enough to coat the back of the spoon, 5 to 10 minutes.

Old Bay Paloma

I wanted a refreshing citrusy cocktail to complement everything else—but with a local twist. Maryland's hallmark spice blend gives this orange drink a kick. This drink cannot be made in advance, as the soda will lose its bubbles.

Makes 1 drink

INGREDIENTS

¼ cup freshly squeezed lemon juice

1 teaspoon Old Bay Seasoning

Ice

2 ounces tequila

2 ½ ounces orange soda

DIRECTIONS

1. Pour the lemon juice onto a shallow plate and put the Old Bay on another. Dip the rim of a tumbler glass into the lemon juice, then place the wet rim into the Old Bay and turn the glass to coat.

2. Fill the glass with ice, then add the tequila and orange soda. Stir to combine.

5. Remove the saucepan from the heat and add the 2 ¼ cups Pecorino Romano and 2 ¼ cups Gruyère. Mix the cheeses until they melt into the sauce. Add the mustard and 1 tablespoon salt and stir until thoroughly combined.

6. Pour the sauce over the pasta and mix until all of the pasta is completely covered with sauce.

Transfer the pasta to the prepared baking dish, using a rubber spatula to smooth the surface. Sprinkle the remaining 1 tablespoon of each cheese on top, then the panko.

7. Bake until the top is golden brown and bubbling, 5 to 10 minutes. Serve immediately.

ABOVE AND OPPOSITE: Lemons do double duty as place cards. I matched the tablecloth to the lobsters.

Chocolate Meringue Cake

As a self-confessed chocoholic and compulsive taster of pastries, chocolate cake is my thing. I like a chocolate cake that tastes like chocolate but is not too sweet. Inspired by the classic recipe on the Baker's chocolate bar box, I've tinkered with this recipe over many years. The meringue frosting is a dramatic complement.

Makes one (4-layer, 9-inch) cake; serves 8

INGREDIENTS

CAKE

8 large eggs, separated

2 (4-ounce) packages Baker's Semi-Sweet Baking Chocolate Bars

4 cups all-purpose flour

2 teaspoons baking soda

1 teaspoon kosher salt

4 sticks (1 pound) unsalted butter, softened

4 cups granulated sugar

2 teaspoons vanilla extract

2 cups buttermilk

FROSTING

1½ cups pasteurized egg whites, from a carton

3 cups granulated sugar

DIRECTIONS

MAKE THE CAKE:

1. Preheat the oven to 350°F. Spray two 9-inch round cake pans with canola oil spray.

2. In a stand mixer with the whisk attachment, whisk the egg whites on medium until they form stiff peaks, about 10 minutes. Place the egg whites in a clean bowl and set aside. Clean the stand mixer bowl.

3. Break up the chocolate bars, and put the chocolate chunks in a microwave-safe bowl. Melt in 30-second increments on normal power, stirring well after each increment, until fully melted, 1 to 2 minutes. Slowly add 1 cup lukewarm water. Stir the melted chocolate and water until combined. Set aside.

4. In a medium bowl, whisk the flour, baking soda, and salt.

5. Place the butter and sugar in the bowl of a stand mixer fitted with the paddle attachment and beat on medium speed until fluffy, about 3 minutes. Reduce the speed to low and gradually add the following ingredients in this sequence: the egg yolks, one at a time, the vanilla extract, then the melted chocolate mixture.

6. With the mixer still on low speed, add half the flour mixture and thoroughly combine. Then add half of the buttermilk until combined. Repeat with the remaining flour and buttermilk and beat until fully incorporated.

7. Use a rubber spatula to gently fold the egg whites into the batter. Divide the batter among the prepared pans and bake until a toothpick inserted in the center of each cake comes out clean, about 30 minutes.

8. Allow the cakes to cool for 15 minutes, then remove from the pans and place on parchment-lined baking sheets to cool completely, 1 to 2 hours.

MAKE THE FROSTING:

1. Fill a small saucepan three quarters full with water and set over high heat to boil.

2. Put the egg whites and sugar in the metal bowl of a stand mixer. (Using a metal bowl is important as a glass bowl might shatter.)

3. Once the water comes to a boil, set the metal bowl on top of the pot; the water should not touch the bottom of the bowl (if it does, carefully discard some of the water). Over the homemade double boiler, whisk the egg whites and sugar until the sugar dissolves, 5 to 10 minutes. You can check doneness by putting a dab on your fingertip and rubbing it between your fingers to be sure there are no perceptible sugar granules.

4. Return the bowl to the mixer stand fitted with the whisk attachment and mix on low speed until the egg mixture is opaque, 10 to 15 minutes. Increase the speed to high and whisk until stiff peaks form, about 5 minutes.

TO ASSEMBLE THE CAKE:

1. Place one cake on a cake stand. Spread a layer of the meringue frosting on top of the cake. Top with the remaining cake.

2. Use a butter knife to completely cover both layers in the remaining meringue frosting. Once the cake is covered, dip your clean fingers into the meringue. Your fingertips will create the pointy tips.

3. The cake is perfect as if, but if you have a blow torch and would like to create a more dramatic look, brown the tips, keeping the flame 2 to 3 inches away from the meringue tips.

Note: If served on a hot day, refrigerate until ready to serve, up to 12 hours in advance.

Botanical Brunch

For Mother's Day, a bridal or baby shower, or just to celebrate an abundant garden, a flower-filled party is a lovely idea. For the ultimate decor, even better is planning it at the time when your garden is in bloom. I have hosted this brunch multiple times when the forsythia or rhododendron is flowering, but you can plan around whatever flowers bloom in your garden—and set your table beside them.

The tablecloth makes a party in and of itself, as it incorporates many familiar spring and summer flowers. You can choose table linens that harmonize with the flowers or choose flowers based on your table linens. I love matchy-matchy, so I went with napkins that were the same as my Pressed Flower tablecloth. The real flowers were a three-dimensional version of the two-dimensional covering, bringing the table to life. The glasses and candles came in the same colors as many of the flowers, so they were complementary as well.

The table is over-the-top flowers in the best way, from the dramatic tablecloth and napkins to the lovely floral arrangements. The surrounding garden accentuates the botanical theme.

Edible flowers are a fun party trick and can be added to most menu items, from eggs to ice cream. They can be tricky to find, but many specialty food stores can procure them with advance notice. Otherwise, you can grow them in your own backyard; pansies, nasturtium, dandelions, and lilac are quite accessible—just be sure not to use pesticides! In this menu, edible flowers float on cocktails, fold into summer rolls, garnish green salads, and bake into cookies. You could also freeze edible flowers into popsicles and bake them into breads.

My outfit coordinated with the theme, of course. Earrings featured tiny pink pressed flowers, and my dress (an Etsy find) continued the pattern with its embroidered patches.

Ralph Waldo Emerson said, "Earth laughs in flowers." The saturated colors of flowers and their manifold shapes are some of the most beautiful natural phenomena—and their evolutionary beauty is something to celebrate.

PREVIOUS PAGES, OPPOSITE, AND ABOVE: The Chefanie Pressed Flower napkins and tablecloth, along with actual flower arrangements and garden setting, create an all-encompassing floral experience. White plates keep things balanced and grounded, a contrast with the bounty of color on the table.

Gardener's Spritz

This cocktail with botanical notes is garnished with edible flowers—and makes a lovely party opener.

Makes 8 drinks

INGREDIENTS

12 ounces gin

4 ounces apricot liqueur

4 ounces freshly squeezed lemon juice

Ice

About 24 edible, food-grade flowers, such as bachelor's button, calendula, dianthus, marigold, or pansies, from a specialty food store

DIRECTIONS

1. Before guests arrive, combine the gin, apricot liqueur, and lemon juice in a pitcher and stir. Refrigerate until ready to serve, up to 1 day in advance.

2. For each drink, fill a cocktail shaker with ice and add 2 ½ ounces of the cocktail mixture. Shake, then strain into a colorful drinking glass.

3. Garnish with edible flowers and serve.

THIS PAGE AND OPPOSITE: Edible flowers are used in cocktails atop a stylized cherry blossom linen coaster. Earrings contain pressed flowers and gold flakes. Creating a showstopper of a cake—homemade or store-bought—is easily done with edible flowers.

Flower Spring Rolls

A beloved appetizer because it's healthy, delicious, and pretty. The dipping sauce can be made up to 2 weeks in advance and stored in an airtight container in the fridge.

Makes 24 rolls; serves 8

INGREDIENTS
DIPPING SAUCE

½ cup smooth peanut butter, preferably natural

¼ cup soy sauce or tamari, plus more to taste

2 tablespoons unseasoned rice vinegar, plus more to taste

1 tablespoon honey, plus more to taste

1 tablespoon toasted sesame oil

½ teaspoon finely grated fresh ginger

1 small garlic clove, minced

SPRING ROLLS

At least 48 edible flowers, such as bachelor's button, calendula, dianthus, marigold, or pansies

5 carrots, peeled and cut into matchsticks (approximately 3 cups)

1 head red cabbage, thinly sliced (approximately 3 cups)

48 chives, trimmed to the length of the spring roll

1 (12-ounce) package round rice paper spring roll wrappers

DIRECTIONS

Make the dipping sauce: Combine the peanut butter, soy sauce, rice vinegar, honey, sesame oil, ginger, and garlic in a medium bowl. Taste and adjust the soy sauce, vinegar, and honey, as desired. Transfer to a serving bowl and serve alongside the spring rolls.

MAKE THE SPRING ROLLS:

1. As the spring rolls have to be made quickly to avoid drying out, put the flowers, carrots, cabbage, and chives in individual bowls to have close at hand.

2. Fill a baking sheet that is wide enough to hold the rice paper wrapper with warm water.

3. Hydrate one rice paper wrapper in the water for 10 to 15 seconds, until soft and pliable.

4. Place the wet rice paper wrapper on a slightly dampened cutting board. In the center of the wrapper, place a line of 1 to 3 edible flowers, pretty side face down on the wrapper. (This will ensure that the colorful flowers are maximally visible when the spring roll is wrapped up.)

5. Add bundles of carrots, cabbage, and chives on top of the line of flowers to create a hearty spring roll.

6. To create a tight roll, start wrapping from the edge closest to you. Then fold the outer edges inward. Finally, finish wrapping the spring roll.

7. Transfer to a platter and cover with a damp paper towel. Repeat to create 11 more spring rolls. The spring rolls will keep for 1 to 2 hours at room temperature without becoming brittle.

8. When ready to serve, halve the spring rolls on a bias, arrange them on a platter with the cut side facing out, and present with the dipping sauce.

Flower Cookies

These pretty cookies invite excitement and lots of pictures.

Makes 24 cookies

INGREDIENTS

3 cups all-purpose flour, plus more for dusting

1 ½ teaspoons kosher salt

½ teaspoon baking powder

2 ½ sticks (20 tablespoons) unsalted butter (cut into ½-inch cubes), softened

1 cup sugar

1 large egg

1 large egg yolk

1 teaspoon vanilla extract

Edible flowers and petals, such as bachelor's button, calendula, dianthus, marigold, or pansies

DIRECTIONS

1. In a medium bowl, whisk together the flour, salt, and baking powder.

2. Put the butter and sugar in the bowl of a stand mixer fitted with the paddle attachment and beat on medium speed until creamed, 3 to 5 minutes. Beat in the egg, egg yolk, and vanilla until incorporated.

3. Add one third of the flour mixture to the bowl and beat over low speed to incorporate. Add the remaining flour mixture, in 2 additions, and beat to incorporate.

4. Dust a work surface with flour. Transfer the dough to the work surface. Halve the dough, use your hands to roll each half into balls, and wrap each ball with plastic wrap. Allow the dough balls to chill in the refrigerator for at least 2 hours and up to 3 days.

5. Preheat the oven to 325°F. Line 2 baking sheets with parchment paper.

6. Allow the balls of dough to sit at room temperature for about 5 minutes before rolling. Dust a work surface with flour. Using a rolling pin, roll the dough to a ¼-inch thickness. Use a 2 ½-inch round cookie cutter to cut the dough into about 12 rounds and transfer to one of the prepared baking sheets. Repeat with the remaining dough ball. Gently press a flower into each round.

7. Bake until the edges are a slight golden brown, 12 to 15 minutes.

8. Allow the cookies to cool for 10 to 15 minutes on the baking sheets. Then arrange on a platter to serve or store in an airtight container for up to 3 days.

THIS PAGE: Single sunflowers in bud vases are a lovely floral touch.
OPPOSITE: Edible pansies sourced from a specialty food store dress up simple sugar cookies.

MENU

Follow The Sun
Grilled Sunflower
Roasted Vegetables
Seed-Encrusted Tuna
Sautéed Sunflower Leaves
Sunflower Cake

Sunflower Celebration

For me, sunflowers are the ultimate symbol of summer and, therefore, bliss. These bright yellow flowers, which spend their days turning to face the sun, bring me so much joy as well as nostalgia. When I think of my summers as a little girl, I think of the bunches of fresh blooms at farm stands on Long Island, as well as endless fields in Europe, experienced from the back seat during family trips.

I always wanted to plan a beautiful dinner in a field of sunflowers. The backdrop they create is sure to make guests smile. I incorporated this happy plant into all elements of the decor, from the shape of the cocktail napkins and place mats to the folds of the table napkins. As seat assignments, I wrote each guest's name on individual

At the pinnacle of summer, yellow sunflowers are at their most bountiful and least expensive. I incorporated fresh flowers with decorative versions on linens and plates. At each seat is a small bag of sunflower seeds. Guests can either munch on them or plant them to grow their own sunflowers.

pouches of sunflower seeds—a keepsake of the event. The silver-plated cups had little sunflowers engraved on them. The table was an homage to the iconic flower, emphasizing its yellow color; the tablecloth featured yellow flowers, and the floral centerpiece was a continuous runner of Oasis floral foam covered with sunflowers.

Sunflowers are unusual plants in that all parts are edible, from the stalk to the petals, head, and seeds. Similar to artichokes, sunflowers have meaty hearts that can be sautéed. The stalks (more tender toward the head) can be eaten like celery. Leaves can be used like spinach sautéed with garlic. Petals are a lovely garnish for anything from ice cubes to cocktails and dessert. I have used sunflower seeds to add crunch to salads, to garnish soups, and to sprinkle on top of breads before baking.

You could add even more interpretations of this special flower, by making flower crowns or putting them in gentlemen's pocket squares. And you can certainly pull this together in your own backyard, regardless of whether you grow them yourself.

ABOVE: A floral runner is a long, low arrangement that does not obstruct conversation at a dining table. This one is easy to make with sunflowers. **OPPOSITE:** I set the table in a field of sunflowers on Long Island, but this party could also be hosted in a backyard garden with homegrown or purchased blooms.

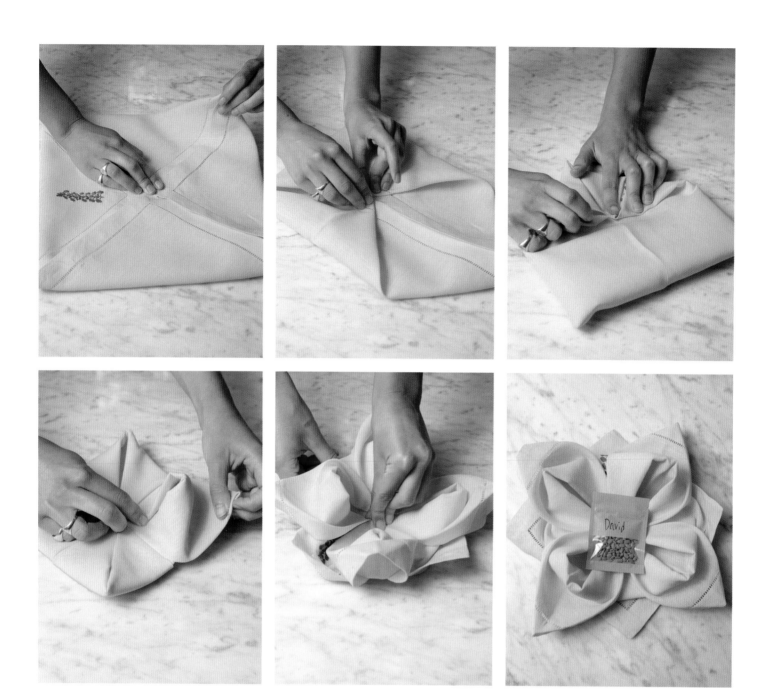

HOW TO MAKE
Sunflower Napkins
To fold a napkin into the shape of a sunflower with 8 points:

1. Open your napkin to its full square shape.

2. Fold the 4 corners into the center of the napkin.

3. Fold the 4 new corners into the center.

4. Carefully flip the napkin over and fold the 4 corners into the center.

5. From behind each corner, pull up the pointed piece underneath to make a petal.
Do this on each corner to create 4 petals.

6. In between each corner piece, pull from behind to create 4 more petals.
You can now place a seat assignment or plate in the middle of each napkin.

Follow the Sun

In keeping with the botanical theme, this cocktail uses elderflower liqueur.

Makes 8 drinks

INGREDIENTS

Edible sunflower petals frozen in ice cubes, for serving

16 ounces tequila

4 ounces elderflower liqueur

4 ounces freshly squeezed lime juice

Ice, for shaking

DIRECTIONS

1. At least 1 day before serving, make the sunflower-petal ice cubes by filling up ice cube trays with water and placing a petal on top of each cube.

2. Before the event, up to 1 day in advance, combine the tequila, liqueur, and lime juice in a pitcher. Stir to combine, then refrigerate until ready to serve, up to 12 hours in advance.

3. For each cocktail, fill a cocktail shaker with regular ice and add 3 ounces of the cocktail mixture. Shake, then strain into a tumbler or julep cup.

4. Garnish with a sunflower petal ice cube.

HOW TO MAKE

Sunflower Table Runner

Purchase 4 bricks of 9-inch Oasis floral foam (see Resources). Gauge the approximate number of sunflowers you'll need based on the surface area of the floral foam and the size of each bloom; I used about 20-25 sunflowers per block. Buy a few more blooms than you think you need. Dunk the Oasis rectangles in water until they are saturated. Arrange the floral foam in a line down the table, leaving room for place settings at both edges. Depending on how much you want to protect your table and tablecloth, you can also create the runner on a wood plank to then place on the table. Prepare each flower by cutting all but 2 inches of each stem. Insert stems into the floral foam until the foam is covered. You can use this method for other flowers like hydrangeas.

Grilled Sunflower

When I first read about the concept of cooking a whole flower head, I was intrigued by the beautiful savory dish. Flowers for dinner? Count me in, always. Plus, it tasted like a nutty version of corn. Sunflowers from your flower store are probably not safe to eat, so instead buy from an organic farmstand—or use sunflowers grown in your own garden without pesticides.

Serves 8

INGREDIENTS

8 young, organic sunflower heads

Olive oil

Kosher salt

DIRECTIONS

1. Clip the sunflowers from their stalks. Remove the tiny little flowers ("disk florets") from the face of the sunflower. Remove the colored petals.

2. Preheat your grill to medium-high or set a large grill pan over medium-high heat.

3. Drizzle each sunflower face with olive oil and season with salt.

4. Set the sunflowers, face down, on the grill or in the pan and cook until the back of the flower is easily pierced with a knife, 5 to 10 minutes.

5. Plate and serve immediately.

Sunflower Cake with Sunflower Petals

A reinterpretation of my classic almond cake with sunflower elements. It happens to be gluten-free!

Makes one (10-inch) cake; serves 8

INGREDIENTS

Sunflower oil for greasing

1 ½ cups shelled sunflower seeds

1 ½ cups sifted confectioners' sugar

1 large egg white, lightly beaten, at room temperature

¾ cup granulated sugar

1 stick (8 tablespoons) unsalted butter, softened

2 teaspoons vanilla extract

6 large eggs

½ cup sunflower seed flour

½ teaspoon baking powder

1 teaspoon kosher salt

Organic sunflower petals and sunflower seeds for garnish

DIRECTIONS

1. Preheat the oven to 325°F and grease a 10-inch springform pan with sunflower oil.

2. Place the sunflower seeds and confectioners' sugar into the bowl of a food processor and pulse to create a grainy paste. This should be very well processed so that there are no little bits of seed. Transfer to a bowl and fold in the egg white with a rubber spatula. There will be extra paste, and it can be stored up to 1 week in the refrigerator and used in lieu of almond paste for pastries.

3. In the bowl of a stand mixer with the paddle attachment, combine ¾ cup of the sunflower paste with the granulated sugar and beat on medium to create a grainier paste, 3 to 5 minutes.

4. Add the butter and vanilla extract and beat on medium speed until the batter is smooth and fluffy, 3 to 5 minutes. Beat in the eggs, one at a time, mixing thoroughly with each additional.

5. In a small bowl, whisk together the sunflower seed flour, baking powder, and salt.

6. Beat the flour mixture into the wet batter in 2 or 3 additions on low speed. Mix just to combine after each addition.

7. Once the mixture is smooth and creamy, pour into the prepared cake pan.

8. Bake for 30 minutes, then place sunflower petals on the surface of the cake in the shape of a sunflower. Bake until the top becomes golden-brown and a toothpick inserted in the center comes out clean, another 15 to 30 minutes.

9. Let the cake cool in the pan for at least 15 minutes before releasing from the pan.

10. Transfer to a cake stand and garnish with sunflower seeds and additional petals. The cake can be served both warm and at room temperature.

Menu

Spanish stuffed dates
Grilled Artichokes
Mixed Empanadas

Seafood Paella
Vegetarian Paella

Skillet Cookies

Beach Bonfire

Eating on the beach by the ocean is a favorite treat of summer. When the sun sets late at the peak of summer, we can watch whales and dolphins swimming off the shore in East Hampton; it definitely beats a TV dinner. We gather beach chairs with picnic foods like pasta salad and fried chicken—or we might grill burgers and hot dogs over a bonfire, to be followed by s'mores. On special occasions, we have clam bakes. Every summer we relish these gatherings, but last summer I really wanted to wow my people with a unique meal on the beach.

Paella is a traditional Spanish seafood dish. Its central ingredient, rice, brings people together: it is eaten all over the world and is common to many cultures. My favorite teacher in culinary school showed me pictures of the paellas he created over open fires by the sea in Spain. He explained how the salt air made the dish more delicious. I knew I had to re-create the concept for my own beach party.

For this summer beach party, we made giant paellas. The salty sea air made this dish even more delicious.

For this party we created two different kinds of paella: seafood and vegetable. We had traditional Spanish tapas (appetizers) to start. I wanted to make a dessert over the fire that was not s'mores. My chocolate chip cookie recipe is beloved, so I adapted it for al fresco preparation. I put my signature cookie dough batter into individual-size cast-iron skillets, to be cooked over the open fire. These skillet cookies were very different from the traditional baked cookies, but everyone loved them.

The visual inspiration was a painting that I had seen at an art fair in Mexico City. Its earthy tones were complementary to the natural colors of the landscape. Anticipating how dark it gets on the beach on a night with only a sliver of a moon, we lit lots of candles in hurricanes on the table and put tiki torches in the sand around the perimeter of the party area. When you host outside, you should check the moon phase and sunset time to plan your lighting. We also used special tablecloth clips (see Resources) that are inexpensive and extremely helpful for outdoor events.

PREVIOUS PAGES: We set a long table in the sand on my favorite beach in East Hampton. Anticipating the darkness of the beach after sunset, we placed candles in hurricanes and battery-operated lamps in between flowers. **ABOVE:** Guests mingle while enjoying sangria punch. **OPPOSITE:** Folding napkins distinctively—like this one in the shape of a scallop shell—is one more way to highlight the party's theme. A spare approach to the floral pieces, in muted tones, complements the casual beach vibe.

Michae

Menu

Spanish stuffed dates
Grilled Artichokes
Mixed Empanadas

Seafood Paella
Vegetarian Paella

Skillet Cookies

OPPOSITE AND ABOVE: The place setting celebrates the seafood theme with Chefanie scallop-shaped place mats and shell-decorated flatware. Each place card is embellished with bits of shells, rocks, and driftwood collected on the beach before the party.

THIS PAGE: Sangria is served in a vintage punch bowl with lots of ice. OPPOSITE: Appetizers included mixed empanadas. We hung fans from each seat using clear fish wire; the fans served a dual purpose of decoration and function.

Stone Fruit Sangria Punch

This is an American summer twist on the traditional Spanish drink. At the peak of summer, peaches, plums, nectarines, and cherries are at their best, adding a distinctive sweetness.

Makes 24 drinks

INGREDIENTS

4 bottles rosé, chilled

1 (375-ml) bottle elderflower liqueur

2 plums, pitted and sliced into 8 wedges

2 nectarines, pitted and sliced into 8 wedges

2 white peaches, pitted and sliced into 8 wedges

2 yellow peaches, pitted and sliced into 8 wedges

3 cups cherries, pitted and halved

DIRECTIONS

In a punch bowl, combine all ingredients 12 to 24 hours before the event. Refrigerate until ready to serve. Serve with a ladle, chunky ice cubes, and lots of cups!

Paella

This dish is a balanced meal in and of itself, with meat, vegetables, and rice all cooked together. This recipe is written for cooking on a kitchen stove, but it can be cooked over a grill at the beach. If you don't have a paella pan, use an extra-large skillet (at least 16 inches).

Serves 16

INGREDIENTS

1 ¼ cups olive oil

4 large onions, finely chopped

4 garlic cloves, minced

4 tomatoes, peeled (see page 68) and chopped

4 teaspoons paprika

1 teaspoon saffron threads

Kosher salt

8 cups paella rice

12 to 16 cups low-sodium chicken stock

1 (750-ml) bottle dry white wine, such as sauvignon blanc

2 pounds boneless, skinless chicken breasts, cut into 16 (1-inch) chunks

32 clams, soaked in water to purge of grit, and scrubbed

32 mussels, scrubbed and debearded

1 (10-ounce) bag frozen peas

12 ounces Spanish-style chorizo, cut into ½-inch-thick rounds

2 pounds extra-large shrimp, peeled and deveined

4 cups peeled diced potatoes, boiled and seasoned with salt and lemon juice (optional)

DIRECTIONS

1. Warm the oil in a large skillet or paella pan set over medium heat. Add the onions and cook until soft and translucent, 5 to 7 minutes. Add the garlic, tomatoes, paprika, saffron, and 1 ½ teaspoons salt and cook until the tomatoes soften, a few minutes more.

2. Using a wooden spoon, stir in the rice, being sure to coat thoroughly in the mixture. Pour 12 cups of the chicken stock and all of the wine over the rice and stir. Increase the heat to medium-high and bring to a boil; season with salt.

3. Stir the mixture, spreading the rice evenly in the pan. Reduce the heat to medium and cook for 10 minutes, until the rice is al dente, stirring to move the rice constantly.

4. Add the chicken and allow to cook for 8 to 10 minutes, turning occasionally so the pieces cook evenly. If the rice seems dry, add the rest of the stock.

5. Add the clams and mussels and cook for 10 minutes; discard any that are not open after this time.

6. Add the peas and mix until cooked through, about 1 minute.

7. Add the chorizo, ensuring it has some chance to brown on the bottom of the pan, about 1 minute.

8. Add the shrimp and cook, turning once, until opaque and pink, about 3 minutes.

9. If using potatoes, add them and cook until warmed through.

10. Serve immediately. To plate individual servings, place some rice on a plate as a base and add a sampling of the chicken, shellfish, sausage, and potatoes (if using) on top. This will highlight all of the variety in the dish.

Skillet Cookies

I adapted this recipe for outdoor cooking. You can use this method over an open fire at the beach or on a grill for a barbecue. Of course, you can also bake them in the oven at home. The browned butter in this recipe gives the cookies a special caramelized taste.

Serves 16

INGREDIENTS

1 ¾ sticks (14 tablespoons) unsalted butter, plus more for skillets

1 ¾ cups all-purpose flour

½ teaspoon baking soda

¾ cup packed dark brown sugar

½ cup granulated sugar

2 teaspoons vanilla extract

1 teaspoon kosher salt

1 large egg

1 large yolk

1 ¼ cups semisweet chocolate chips or chunks

Vanilla ice cream

DIRECTIONS

1. If baking in the oven, preheat the oven to 375°F. If cooking over open fire, carefully set a grate over an open fire. If cooking on a grill, set to medium heat and close the lid.

2. Butter 16 (3 ½-inch) cast-iron skillets.

3. Whisk together the flour and baking soda in medium bowl. Set aside.

4. Melt 1 ¼ sticks (10 tablespoons) of the butter in a 10-inch skillet over medium-high heat (avoid using a nonstick skillet to brown butter as it's hard to gauge the color of the butter). Continue cooking, swirling the pan constantly, until the butter is dark golden brown, 1 to 3 minutes.

5. Transfer the browned butter to a large heatproof bowl. Add the remaining 4 tablespoons butter and stir until completely melted.

6. Add the brown sugar, granulated sugar, vanilla, and salt to the melted butter. Whisk until fully incorporated. Add the egg and yolk. Whisk until the egg is fully incorporated and the mixture is smooth with no sugar lumps, about 30 seconds.

7. Let the mixture stand for 3 minutes, then whisk for 30 seconds. Repeat this process 2 more times until the mixture is thick, smooth, and shiny.

8. Use a rubber spatula to incorporate the flour mixture into the butter-sugar mixture until just combined. Fold in chocolate chips.

9. Give the dough a final stir to ensure that there are no flour pockets.

10. Distribute the cookie dough evenly among the skillets. If baking in the oven, put the skillets on baking sheets (for easier transporting to and from the oven) and bake for 12 to 15 minutes, until the middle is set. If cooking over open fire, place the skillets at the edges of the grate, where the flames are lower (the center of the grate will be too hot and the cookies will burn). Cook 25 to 30 minutes, until the middle is set. If cooking on a grill, place the skillets on the middle grate. Close the lid. Cook 15 to 20 minutes, until the middle is set.

11. Use high-heat oven mitts to transfer the skillets to plates that can endure the hot temperature. Serve warm with ice cream.

Holiday Parties

The holidays are sacred—religiously, culturally, socially. The traditions associated with celebrating them keep families and communities together. In the darkest days of the year, we light up our cities with markets serving sweetened hot chocolate and cookies, and we light up our homes with twinkling lights and candles. On the longest days of summer, towns across America celebrate the Fourth of July with parades and flag cakes. Holidays provide us with something to anticipate with excitement, something to unite around, something to enjoy.

Bringing these celebrations into your home allows for a deeply personal, totally unique interpretation for a more intimate group of favorite people. These at-home traditions are largely intertwined with food and decor. Special china, desserts, and candles contribute to creating a net of magic that makes the holidays so indelible in our minds. More than any other hosted gatherings, holidays are such special occasions that no shortcuts can be taken—from fresh homemade breads to the best cuts of meat, slow-cooked, to elaborate, ample desserts. Often these recipes become part of family traditions and important memories.

The key to hosting holidays is to broadly think about each holiday's essence, including its hallmark colors, decorative elements, and dishes; select your favorite aspects among them, then add your own twist where possible. For a winter celebration, I extended the holiday plaids from the table linens to doughnuts, cookies, and cakes. New Year's Eve is often a time to dress up, so I fancied up my chocolate-dipped strawberries in miniature tuxedos. The table was inspired by disco balls that might illuminate a dance party, including miniature disco-ball-shaped place card holders. Each holiday has its own iconic identity, but you should feel free to embellish.

By my barometer of joy, holiday parties rank the highest. My only rule: have fun!

Menu

POINSETTIA WREATH

ALMOND PINECONE

VERTICAL PEAR SALAD

CROWN ROAST

POMMES DAUPHINES

POINSETTIA COOKIES

PLAID DONUTS

Festive Fête

Regardless of the holiday you celebrate, it seems like the whole world is in a festive spirit in December. A lovely way to revel in the season is by hosting a holiday meal. The meal in this chapter is inspired by classic Christmas dishes but is also generally festive. Poinsettia, the iconic red winter flower, inspires the shape of a cheesy red appetizer and cookies. The pine-cone-shaped mound of soft cheeses is an example of how presentation alone can wow guests. A crown roast is one of the most grand dishes and is suitably hearty for the cold weather. A simple green salad is presented in between layers of pear to spark visual intrigue.

Classic holiday motifs are incorporated into the menu. Touches of plaid, shades of green and navy, and winter leafage decorate the table. The tablecloth pattern features traditional winter motifs such as antlers, bells, and holly . . . and gets a zhuzh with tins of caviar.

Grandpa

Christmas Dinner

Baked Brie with Cranberries

Beef Wellington

Pommes Dauphines

Roasted Brussels Sprouts

Wild Rice

Honey Mushrooms

Tuile Cookies

Peppermint Croquembouche

Yellow Cake

Classic motifs are sprinkled across the table. Red and green dominate. On and around the tablescape, there are plaids in a variety of formats: tartan plaids are printed on linens and crackers to adorn the table; doughnuts and cakes also boast this pattern; even my outfit, down to the tartan barrette in my hair, matches the rest. The abundance of plaids creates a visual cohesion. Centerpiece and food garnishes include cedar clippings snipped from my backyard. Other local greens could be substituted, but the scent of this decorative vegetation emphasizes the wintry theme.

A holiday party is the time to invest as much time and money as possible; it's the season to be generous. Take the time to cook long recipes and iron out the wrinkles in your tablecloth. Buy the best ingredients that you can afford, from good cheeses to champagne. If you can find a source for live music, book it. Otherwise, research a great playlist. Most important of all, though, is inviting as many people as you can. There's no other season in which the phrase "the more, the merrier" rings truer.

PREVIOUS PAGES: This menu frame features flowers from antique prints, reformatted digitally. The color palette here evokes Christmas without being completely red and green. The place setting is from Chefanie, including the tablecloth, place mat, plates, napkin, flatware, and glassware. OPPOSITE AND ABOVE: There are so many ways to set a holiday table. Plaid sets the perfect tone; depending on your appetite for the pattern, it can be used selectively or all over.

Dishes from different courses—appetizers, entrées, and dessert— mingle on the table, allowing guests to indulge in whatever they feel like.

Almond Pine Cone

I love anything trompe l'oeil, but especially a mound of cheese dressed up like a pine cone. This pine cone can stand alone or be part of a wider wintry cheeseboard. It's easiest to create this directly on the serving platter to avoid casualties in transit.

Serves 8

INGREDIENTS

2 (8-ounce) blocks cream cheese, softened to room temperature

6 ounces goat cheese, softened to room temperature

1 tablespoon chopped thyme

1 teaspoon kosher salt

½ teaspoon freshly ground black pepper

2 cups almonds

3 sprigs rosemary

Crackers, for serving, such as Original Triscuits or Lesley Stowe's Raincoast Chips

DIRECTIONS

1. Prepare your serving platter.

2. Put the cream cheese, goat cheese, thyme, salt, and pepper in the bowl of a stand mixer with the paddle attachment. Beat on medium speed until thoroughly incorporated, about 5 minutes.

3. On the prepared baking sheet, mold the mixture into an oval shape with one pointy tip, mimicking the shape of an actual pine cone.

4. Starting at the bottom of the pointy tip, insert the first almond (pointy side out). Work your way around the pine cone from the pointy tip to the rounded side. Make rows of almonds around the entire shaped cheese until the whole mound is covered. Insert rosemary sprigs at the top.

5. You can serve immediately, or cover and refrigerate until ready to serve, up to 2 days in advance. Serve with sturdy crackers.

Vertical Salads

Reimagine your favorite salads in a vertical format. This is a traditional pear and arugula salad with slivered almonds, goat cheese, and herbs—arranged within a full pear for a surprising and unique presentation. The pear is cut horizontally into three pieces: The top of the fruit with stem is cut off, then the pear is cored; the bottom part of the pear is cut crosswise into two more pieces and salad ingredients are inserted in between these pieces. The stem piece is placed back on the top.

You can also apply this technique to other produce to suit the season: Summer tomatoes can be sliced, filled with mozzarella and basil, and drizzled with balsamic reduction. Autumn apples can be filled with a dressed mix of crushed walnuts, spinach, sliced red onion, and feta. Or, in the winter, a roasted acorn squash can be loaded with a lemony rice.

Poinsettia Wreath

The saltiness of the cheese, the sweetness of the cranberry sauce, and the melty warmth of the whole dish make it irresistible.

Serves 8

INGREDIENTS

1 sheet frozen puff pastry, thawed

4 tablespoons cranberry sauce, ideally homemade but if using a can, warm it so it's more easily spreadable

8 (¼-inch-thick, 1 ½-inch-wide) slices Brie

1 ½ tablespoons grated pistachio nuts

1 large egg, beaten

Chopped fresh herbs, optional for garnish

DIRECTIONS

1. Preheat the oven to 350°F. Line a large baking sheet with parchment paper.

2. Unroll the puff pastry dough onto the prepared baking sheet. Within the rectangular pastry sheet, carve a circle about 10 inches in diameter and discard the scraps.

In the center of the circle, carve a star shape with 8 points. The points should be long and narrow so they can partially cover the filling and touch the opposite side of the circle. Discard the center star.

3. Spread the cranberry sauce all over the puff pastry circle (but not on the star points), and add slices of brie where they will be nestled once the star shapes cover them. Sprinkle pistachio over the cranberry sauce and Brie.

4. Bring the star points outward, over a slice of Brie and the filling, to the outer edge of the puff pastry round. Press together, so that the dough sticks. Continue with all of the star points until a wreath shape is formed.

5. Brush the exposed puff pastry with beaten egg. Bake the wreath until golden brown and puffy, 15 to 20 minutes.

6. Garnish with herbs, if desired. Cut it into 8 pieces so that each piece includes a piece of Brie. Serve while still warm.

Scarlet Swizzle

The natural color of cranberry, bubbles in champagne, and fragrance of rosemary create the jovial alchemy that you want in a holiday cocktail.

Makes 10 drinks

INGREDIENTS

½ cup Cointreau

2 cups cranberry juice

1 (750-ml) bottle champagne

¼ cup fresh rosemary leaves

DIRECTIONS

1. Before guests arrive, combine the Cointreau and cranberry juice in a pitcher and stir. Store in the refrigerator until ready to serve, up to 12 hours in advance.

2. When ready to serve, fill a tumbler halfway with the Cointreau and cranberry juice mixture. Top with champagne, garnish with rosemary, and serve.

HOW TO MAKE
Decorating Doughnuts

To decorate doughnuts with the plaid pattern seen opposite, apply our patterned sheets to a doughnut's wet glaze. Many doughnut stores will allow you to purchase extra glaze, and you can dip one side of each doughnut into it. For circles that fit your doughnuts, you can trace circles on the patterned sheets, or use a hot metal cookie cutter to cut them to the exact size. A metal cookie cutter can be heated over the flames in a stove, just use a mitt to protect your hands from getting burned. This treat doubles as decor.

3. Pull a handful of dough and roll it into a 1 ¼-inch-diameter ball, about the size of a golf ball. Place on the baking sheet. Repeat with the remaining dough.

4. Cover the baking sheet with plastic wrap and refrigerate for at least 1 hour and up to 2 hours.

5. Preheat the oven to 375°F. Line a clean baking sheet with parchment paper.

6. Using a sharp knife, make 3 intersecting cuts three quarters of the way into the ball (make sure not to cut all the way through). Separate the 6 wedges and pull down slightly to create the flower petals (the petals will continue to unfurl as the cookies bake). Place each piece onto the prepared baking sheet at least 2 inches apart.

7. Bake until the cookies no longer look wet but before they start to brown, 9 to 11 minutes.

8. Cool on the baking sheet for at least 15 minutes, then arrange on a serving platter. They can be served warm or at room temperature.

Poinsettia Cookies

Here is an idea to create festive red Christmas flower cookies without needing to purchase a cookie cutter!

Makes 12 to 14 cookies

INGREDIENTS

1 ½ sticks (12 tablespoons) unsalted butter, softened

½ cup sugar

1 3-ounce box red (raspberry) Jell-O gelatin

1 large egg

2 cups all-purpose flour

DIRECTIONS

1. Line a baking sheet with parchment paper.

2. In a stand mixer with the paddle attachment, mix the butter, sugar, Jell-O gelatin, and egg on medium speed until creamed, about 5 minutes. Add the flour and mix on low speed until a cookie dough consistency is achieved.

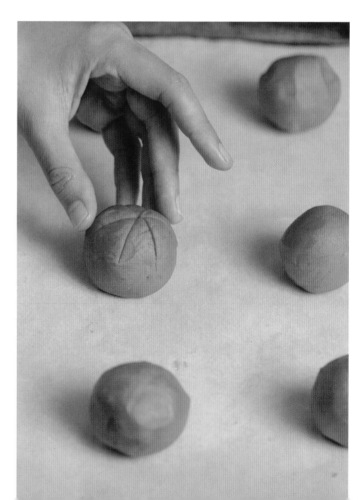

Disco Wonderland

No theme gets me in the party mood more than disco. Even though its heyday has passed, everyone enjoys a disco-themed party. I especially love it for New Year's Eve; in my mind, it is everything the last night of the year should be.

The disco ball itself is the most fun prop ever. It informed the silvery sparkly decor of the table, from the tablecloth to the candles to the serving platters. Silver spray paint makes anything disco. We went to town, transforming faux hydrangeas and fruit into glittery table decor. We brought the appetizer board into the theme with an edible disco ball: after molding soft cheese into a round ball and applying squares of provolone cheese, we sprayed it with edible silver spray paint (see Resources). Finally, each name was written with a silver paint pen on black cardstock, and then

Silver and black connote elegance, and using these colors as inspiration makes for a stylish way to ring in the New Year. Disco ball earrings match the theme.

each place card went into a miniature disco ball place card holder set on black linen with silver trim.

I leaned into sexy black foods for the main event. The party opener—the snack board—included only dark foods: blackberries, black licorice, charcoal crackers, licorice-flavored popcorn, dark concord grapes, and dried cherries. Sea bass, with its silver and black scales, fit into the theme perfectly, especially because it is a relatively light dish that does not preclude guests from dancing after dinner. The fish was arranged on a plate with black rice. There were manifold options for dessert, including a cake decorated with silver sprinkles, black and white ice creams finished off with black sesame bark, and Black-Tie Strawberries.

More than any other party in this book, music is deeply critical to this one. Short of a funky sixteen-piece band dressed in sparkles, the most authentic route would be to gather vintage disco albums and a turntable.

ABOVE AND OPPOSITE: Hydrangeas and fruits sprayed with silver paint adorn the silver-sequin tablecloth. Place cards are held in disco ball–shaped holders.

ABOVE: You don't have to hire a calligrapher to make eye-catching place cards. Here I wrote names on black cards in a festive silver ink with squiggles and dots. **OPPOSITE:** Squiggles are echoed in the unique napkin and place mat shapes.

2. Before guests arrive, combine the gin, grape juice, and black currant juice in a pitcher and mix with a fork. Refrigerate until ready to serve, up to 12 hours in advance.

3. For each drink, put a spherical ice cube in a tumbler. Pour the drink into the tumbler to three quarters full. Top with club soda and sprinkle with edible silver powder.

Sea Bass with Black Rice

A balanced meal that happens to match the event.

Serves 8

INGREDIENTS

3 cups black rice

Kosher salt

1 tablespoon black pepper

8 (4-ounce) sea bass fillets, skin on

Avocado oil

2 tablespoons minced chives

DIRECTIONS

1. In a medium saucepan over high heat, combine 5 ¼ cups water, the rice, and 3 teaspoon salt. Once boiling, cover, reduce the heat to low, and simmer for 30 minutes. Remove from the heat and let rest for 5 minutes. Fluff with a fork.

2. While the rice cooks, blot the sea bass fillets with paper towels and sprinkle both sides with salt and pepper. Set a large nonstick skillet over medium-high heat. Once hot, add 2 teaspoons oil and swirl it around the pan. Carefully place the fish in the pan, skin side down. Cook until the fillets are white halfway up the side of the fillet, about 3 minutes. Flip and cook on the other side for 3 minutes. (If you need to cook the fillets in batches, put the cooked fillets on a baking sheet lined with parchment paper in a 200°F oven while you cook the remaining fillets. Add another couple teaspoons of oil to the pan.)

3. To plate, fill a small ramekin with rice. Put a serving plate over the ramekin and flip. Remove the ramekin to reveal a neat mound of rice. Place the fish alongside the rice and garnish with chives. Repeat for the remaining servings. Serve immediately.

Boogie Punch

Ice cubes do so much for a cocktail, and these—made in spherical silicone molds—recall the fun of a disco ball.

Makes 8 drinks

INGREDIENTS

8 spherical ice cubes

2 cups gin

1 cup grape juice

1 cup black currant juice

½ cup club soda

Edible silver powder

DIRECTIONS

1. At least 1 day before serving, make the spherical ice cubes by pouring water into the individual pockets of a spherical ice tray.

HOW TO MAKE
Disco Cheeseboard

This is a fun addition to an evening party. The anchor is the disco cheese ball. To make it, I rolled softened goat cheese into a ball and placed it in the middle of a silver serving tray. Following the orientation of an actual disco ball, I covered it with sliced provolone cheese squares. Then, I used edible spray paint to make the whole thing silver. Around it, I filled the tray with dark snacks: black licorice wheels, chocolate-covered cashews, dried cherries, blackberries, licorice-flavored popcorn, sesame crackers, black seedless grapes, and dark chocolate.

ABOVE: Use silver sprinkles to decorate a cake—whether it's homemade or store-bought.
RIGHT: Black sesame brittle is the garnish on black and white ice creams served in old-fashioned sundae glasses.

Black-Tie Strawberries

A festive no-bake dessert for New Year's Eve, weddings, or birthdays.

Serves 8

INGREDIENTS

16 large strawberries of uniform size with stems, washed and dried

1 (12-ounce) bag white chocolate chips

1 tablespoon olive oil

1 (12-ounce) bag black Candy Melts (see Resources)

DIRECTIONS

1. Line a baking sheet with parchment paper.

2. Melt the white chocolate chips in a microwave-safe bowl in 30-second increments, stirring in between each increment, until the white chocolate is completely melted. Stir in 1 ½ teaspoons olive oil.

3. Holding a strawberry by the stem, dip it into the white chocolate so all but the very top with stem is covered in chocolate.

4. Place on the prepared baking sheet, then continue with the remaining strawberries. Allow the white chocolate to harden at room temperature, approximately 1 ½ to 3 hours.

5. Melt the candy melts in a microwave-safe bowl in 30-second increments, stirring in between each increment, until the candy melts are completely liquid. Stir in the remaining 1 ½ teaspoons olive oil.

6. Holding a strawberry by the stem, dip each side into the melted candy melts on a diagonal from the bottom tip to the top edge of the white chocolate. This forms the shape of a tuxedo jacket. Place the strawberry on the baking sheet and continue with the remaining strawberries.

7. Dip a toothpick or skewer into melted candy melts and form little round button and a bow-tie shapes on the tuxedo shirt. Place on the baking sheet and continue with the remaining strawberries.

8. Allow the decorations to harden at room temperature, 2 to 3 hours.

9. Place the strawberries on a serving tray and serve the same day at room temperature.

THIS PAGE: Oreos, chocolate wafers, or other dark cookies can be stacked to create drama; it's like a champagne tower, but kid-friendly and easier to make.

Menu

Cupid's Kiss Cocktail

It Girl Salad

Steak with Heart Frites

Chocolate Fondue

Galentine's Day

February fourteenth is not about date night for me. I love the color palette, though, and it's reason enough to celebrate. As I've grown up, I've realized that it's a perfect opportunity to gather my girlfriends for a Galentine's Day feast. Even if your girl gathering takes place before or after the actual official date, this new holiday is a fun excuse to spoil your friends. Festive candy can provide inspiration as well as humor and a little zhuzh. Beyond that, my planning is all about gushing love for my favorite ladies.

This year my North Star were XO candies I found at Trader Joe's in a range of pinks and reds. I used pink radicchio lettuce in my It Girl Salad; as if by magic, this vegetable is in season at the same time as the holiday. Also my three-tiered chocolate

The center of the table evokes a cottage garden with a tangle of colorful flowers "growing" in all directions out of the moss. Complementary pink, white, and red candies in silver dishes dot the table.

fountain was pink; we used pink food dye to make the melted white chocolate our desired color. Guests were invited to dip strawberries into it. The evening kicked off with a cheese—and chocolate—"board" in a red heart-shaped chocolate box. For the entrée, and as a twist on the classic steak frites, I cut the potatoes into hearts and roasted them. As a party favor, I sent each guest home with a classic heart-shaped box of chocolates from La Maison du Chocolat.

I hosted the party at my friend's beautiful flower shop in Queens. Given the store's nature, the space was already full of flowers; however, we added more to the table—and to each glass. I wanted the table to evoke a miniature field of flowers. We put down moss in between each blossom to represent ground cover. Additionally, pink candles and candies decorated the table: sour lips, pomegranate white chocolate bark, and spicy cinnamon Juju bear gummies. The plates were floral too, and the napkins, with a lipstick-kiss motif, were folded into hearts.

ABOVE: White chocolate bark with pomegranate seeds is an easy-to-make treat for a special day. **OPPOSITE:** In addition to the table, we filled a flower shop with pink flowers, creating a springlike escape from February's cold.

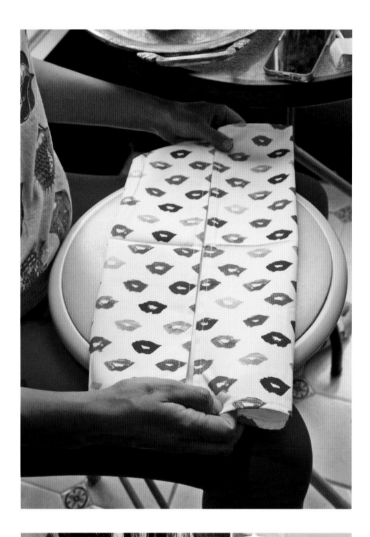

Fold a Heart-Shaped Napkin

Iron a square fabric napkin. Lay it out fully opened with the pattern facing down. Fold the top and bottom edge inward to meet in the middle of the square, so that your napkin is half the width of the original square. Then, fold in half again, so that you have a strip of napkin that is one-quarter the original width. Fold the left side upward toward the center of the napkin, and then do the same with the right side. Fold the inside corners of each side of the strips inward to form a heart shape.

Chocolate Box Cheese Board

As soon as your pharmacy or grocery store gets its seasonal arrival of Valentine's loot, purchase the largest heart-shaped box of chocolates that you can find. Ahead of your party, source things that you would normally put on a cheeseboard: fruits, nuts, and hunks of cheese. Remove some of the chocolate from the chocolate box (they can be repurposed as table snacks or for the dessert buffet), and fill the chocolate box as you would a cheese board.

Cupid's Kiss

The Valentine's Day hallmark food is chocolate, and this delicious cocktail (not pictured) is basically an adult milkshake.

Makes 1 drink

INGREDIENTS

Red sugar sprinkles

2 ounces chocolate syrup, plus more to coat rim

Ice

2 ounces vodka

2 ounces chocolate liqueur

DIRECTIONS

1. Pour chocolate syrup into a shallow dish, and put the red sugar sprinkles on a separate small plate. Dip the rim of the martini glass into the chocolate syrup, then dip into the sprinkles and turn the glass to coat.

2. For each drink, fill a cocktail shaker with ice, 2 ounces of the chocolate syrup, the vodka, and chocolate liqueur. Shake, then strain into the glass.

1. In a small bowl, whisk the honey and the vinegar until the honey dissolves. Add the lemon juice, olive oil, and mustard and whisk to combine.

2. In a large bowl, toss the radicchio, dill, toasted pine nuts, currants, and grated cheese. Add the dressing and toss to coat the leaves. Distribute on 8 salad plates.

HOW TO MAKE

Potato Heart Frites

Use a heart-shaped cookie cutter to cut your potatoes into little hearts. I roast them at 400°F on a parchment-lined baking sheet brushed with olive oil and sprinkled with salt and a little chopped fresh thyme—until there's some caramelization on the sides, about 20 minutes You can serve these with steak, duck, chicken, fish, or whatever other dish your heart desires.

It Girl Salad

The fact that the most perfect pink radicchio is in season over Valentine's Day is not lost on me. The sweetness from the currants and dressing balances the bitterness of the leafy vegetable.

Serves 8

INGREDIENTS

1 tablespoon honey

1 tablespoon champagne vinegar

3 tablespoons freshly squeezed lemon juice

1 tablespoon olive oil

1 teaspoon Dijon mustard

2 heads radicchio rosa (pink radicchio), leaves separated

1 bunch dill, finely chopped

2 tablespoons pine nuts, toasted

2 tablespoons currants

2 tablespoons grated Pecorino Romano

Love Letter Cookies

As much as I love cookie cutters, it's handy to know some cookie folds and shapes that don't require any new or special tools. These sugar cookies shaped like love letters are darling.

Makes 20 cookies

INGREDIENTS

3 cups all-purpose flour, plus more for dusting

1 ½ teaspoons kosher salt

½ teaspoons baking powder

2 ½ sticks (20 tablespoons) butter (cut into ½-inch cubes), softened

1 cup sugar

1 large egg

1 large egg yolk

1 teaspoon vanilla extract

½ cup raspberry jam

DIRECTIONS

1. In a medium bowl, whisk together the flour, salt, and baking powder.

2. Put the butter and sugar in the bowl of a stand mixer fitted with the paddle attachment and beat on medium speed until creamed, 3 to 5 minutes. Beat in the egg, egg yolk, and vanilla until incorporated.

3. Add one third of the flour mixture to the bowl and beat over low speed to incorporate. Add the remaining flour mixture, in 2 additions, and beat to incorporate.

4. Dust a work surface with flour. Transfer the dough to the work surface. Halve the dough, use your hands to roll each half into balls, and wrap each ball with plastic wrap. Allow the dough balls to chill in the refrigerator for at least 2 hours and up to 3 days.

5. Preheat the oven to 325°F. Line 2 baking sheets with parchment paper.

6. Allow the balls of dough to sit at room temperature for about 5 minutes before rolling. Dust a work surface with flour. Using a rolling pin, roll the dough to a ¼-inch thickness.

Using a ruler or other size guide, cut into 20 4 x 4-inch squares.

7. Add a dollop of raspberry jam in the center. Turn the square so it is a diamond and fold the bottom up to the raspberry jam. With dabs of water, wet the outer two corners and fold inward, so only the top corner remains flat. Place on a baking sheet. Repeat with the remaining dough ball.

8. Bake until golden brown on the edges, 12 to 16 minutes. Allow the cookies to cool for 10 to 15 minutes. Arrange on a platter to serve or store in an airtight container for up to 3 days.

THIS PAGE: As a twist on a traditional chocolate fountain, I dyed melted white chocolate pink and poured it into my favorite machine. I'd never seen it before, and guests really enjoyed dipping strawberries, pretzels, and marshmallows into the unique color.

MENU

Seafood Tower
Crab Cakes
Hamburgers
Hot Dogs
Soft Shell Crabs
Potatoes
Pavlova

Fourth of July Jubilee

The Fourth of July kicks off summer and sets the tone for the ensuing season. By that first weekend of July, the days are long and bright. The weather is hot. The kids are out of school and many people schedule vacations. It's a happy time of year.

As with Christmas, there's great precedent for how to decorate for this holiday, as there are so many traditional motifs to include, from patriotic flags to anything red, white, and blue. Moreover, many venues where you might celebrate have a view of some sort of fireworks show, a gratis benefit of hosting a party on the Fourth.

For this party, I crafted a cocktail that can be batched, so you can focus your attention elsewhere during the main event. Grilling burgers and hot dogs does not really allow you much mobility, but if you have help hosting this party you can also include a novelty dish, like soft-shell crabs; this delicacy elevates the whole affair. A seafood tower on ice can be prepared before guests arrive too; however, for safety

Red, white, and blue decorate this patriotic table. For me, this holiday also marks the beginning of summer, which is reason for celebration, too.

purposes, it must be supervised if it is kept outdoors in the summer sun. A solution to this is keeping extra seafood in the refrigerator and replenishing the tower and ice often. A seafood tower is only really safely possible if you're hosting at home where refrigeration is accessible. A pavlova is an easy, light dessert that can be dressed up to look beautiful.

For decor, I plan everything around the flag. It goes without saying that this fête is red, white, and blue. Not only do I incorporate actual flags in the flower arrangements, but I also use bunting-shaped cocktail napkins for each drink. For other Fourth of July parties, I've used crackers and ribbons with a flag pattern. Cookies are edible decor, and I've done multiple iterations of flag cookies. Finally, the Fourth of July feels like a major tablecloth holiday, so grab a large swathe of fabric to dress up your dining or buffet tables.

To get everyone in the spirit, invite guests to wear red, white, and blue.

PREVIOUS PAGES: A blue-and-white starry sky tablecloth is the foundation for fireworks above: red and white linens, blue and white plates, red roses with miniature flags in bud vases, and a stylized flag pattern on the cookies and crackers, all from Chefanie.
ABOVE AND OPPOSITE: An alternative table concept with red block-print poppies and red embroidered linens. I wrapped flag ribbons around candlesticks, but be sure to blow out the flames before they get too close.

ABOVE AND OPPOSITE: As long as you stay with the red, white, and blue color scheme, you can play with different linen patterns and still convey the patriotic feel of the holiday. On the right, I love the touch of yellow in the daisies and mums.

MENU

Seafood Tower
Crab Cakes
Hamburgers
Hot Dogs

Soft Sh

Red, White, and Blue Sangria

This has been my go-to Fourth of July cocktail since it was legal for me to have a cocktail. I love how easy it is to batch, and I love all the fruit!

Makes 8 drinks

INGREDIENTS

1 cup blueberries

1 cup strawberries, thinly sliced

1 (750-ml) bottle dry white wine, such as sauvignon blanc

1 cup vodka

1 cup cranberry juice

Sparkling water

DIRECTIONS

1. Put the blueberries and strawberries in a pitcher. Add the wine, vodka, and cranberry juice and stir to combine. Refrigerate for at least 30 minutes and up to 4 hours before serving.

2. When ready to serve, pour into tumblers and top with a splash of sparkling water.

Fried Soft-Shell Crabs

Soft-shell crabs are in season for a brief blissful moment right around July Fourth. Enjoy them then!

Serves 8

INGREDIENTS

16 large soft-shell crabs, cleaned

6 cups whole milk

4 cups all-purpose flour

8 teaspoons Old Bay Seasoning

2 ½ sticks (20 tablespoons) unsalted butter

4 teaspoons kosher salt

Juice from 4 lemons

6 tablespoons chopped parsley

DIRECTIONS

1. Preheat the oven to 200°F. Line a large baking sheet with parchment paper.

2. Put the soft-shell crabs in a large bowl and cover with the milk. Allow them to soak, refrigerated, for 15 to 20 minutes. Discard the milk.

3. Put the flour on a plate. Dry the crabs with paper towels and sprinkle with the Old Bay. Dredge in the flour and shake off the excess.

4. In a large skillet over medium-high heat, melt 8 tablespoons of the butter. When it begins to foam, lower the heat to medium and put as many crabs as will fit without crowding into the skillet, shell side down. Fry until the first side is golden and crisp, about 3 minutes. Flip and cook for another 3 minutes.

5. Use tongs to transfer the crabs to the prepared baking sheets and season with salt. Keep warm in the oven while you cook more of the crabs.

6. Add 4 tablespoons butter to the pan, cook until foaming, and cook more of the crabs as done previously.

7. When all of the crabs are cooked, add the remaining 8 tablespoons butter to the pan and melt until browned over medium heat. Add the lemon juice and allow to cook for a few seconds so the flavors can meld. Remove from the heat and add half of the parsley.

8. Remove the soft-shell crabs from the oven and arrange 2 crabs on each serving plate. Spoon some sauce over the crabs and garnish with the remaining parsley. Serve immediately.

OPPOSITE: A seafood tower is an extravagant crowd-pleaser; be sure to keep it cold with plenty of ice underneath the shellfish.

Pavlova

This is a Swiss Army knife of a recipe. For the Fourth of July, you can use red and blue berries for a patriotic dessert. At other times of the year, you can substitute seasonal fruit.

Serves 8

INGREDIENTS

6 egg whites

1 teaspoon cream of tartar

1 cup sugar

Whipped cream

Blueberries

Raspberries

DIRECTIONS

1. Preheat the oven to 325°F. Line a large baking sheet with parchment paper.

2. Put the egg whites in the bowl of a stand mixer with the whisk attachment. Whisk on medium speed until the whites get a bit frothy, about 10 minutes. Add the cream of tartar and mix again to incorporate.

3. Add the sugar in a slow stream while the mixer runs at low speed. Continue beating on medium speed until a glossy and thicker mixture is obtained, about 10 minutes. You don't want the egg mixture to be stiff, but you do want it to be thick enough to maintain its shape when you transfer it to the baking sheet.

4. Check to be sure the sugar is fully incorporated by rubbing some of the mixture between your fingertips; you should not feel any sugar granules. If you feel sugar granules, continue mixing.

5. Transfer the mixture to the prepared baking sheet and shape into a 3- to 3½-inch-tall round. Place in the oven and reduce the heat to 225°F.

6. After 90 minutes, carefully touch the meringue to make sure that it is dry and brittle; it should not bounce back. If it is not dry, bake for another 30 minutes.

7. Turn off the oven heat and allow the meringue to bake in the residual heat until the oven is cool.

8. Place the meringue on a serving platter and slather with whipped cream. Decorate with blueberries and raspberries. When ready to serve, plate slices of the meringue with some of the berries.

THIS PAGE: For a festive cheeseboard, use all red, white, and blue elements like berries and marshmallows. You can use a paring knife to cut stars out of cheese slices and hearts out of strawberries.

Resources

CAKE DECORATION

CHEFANIE
chefanie.com
For patterned cake wrappers, among other party items

KEREKES
bakedeco.com
For edible spray paints, fun sprinkles, cookie cutters, piping bags, cake pans of every shape and size

FOOD SOURCES

Savory:

ACME SMOKED FISH
acmesmokedfish.com
For the best smoked salmon

D'ARTAGNAN
dartagnan.com
For duck legs, duck breasts, turkeys

EATALY
(locations nationwide)
eataly.com
For pastas, superior produce, and often year-round, in-store source of edible flowers

KALUSTYAN'S
foodsofnations.com
For specialty ingredients, such as edible dry rose petals, dried fruits, exotic, hard-to-find spices, kataifi dough, mango chutney

KOLIKOF CAVIAR & GOURMET
kolikof.com
For Ossetra caviar and Wagyu beef

MINI TACO SHELLS
minitacoshells.com
For colorful taco shells

RESTAURANTWARE
restaurantware.com
For edible cones

SOGNO TOSCANO
sognotoscano.com
For giant cheese wheels, canned artichokes, other Italian specialties

URBANI TRUFFLES
urbani.com
For fresh white Alba truffles, white truffle and porcini "truffle thrills," black truffle bonbons

WALTER'S HOT DOGS
waltershotdogs.com
goldbelly.com/
walters-hot-dogs
For the best pigs in a blanket

Sweet:

DUCK DONUTS
(locations nationwide)
duckdonuts.com
For fresh, warm doughnuts made to order

LA MAISON DU CHOCOLAT
(locations nationwide)
lamaisonduchocolat.com
For a wide range of chocolate boxes

THE MEADOW
themeadow.com
For specialty chocolate bars

ONEG HEIMISHE BAKERY
goldbelly.com/restaurants/oneg-bakery
For double chocolate babka, challah, hamantaschen, rugelach

TEUSCHER
(locations nationwide)
teuscher.com
For champagne truffles, whimsical gift boxes

ALSO

AMAZON
For Barnabas gold leaf papers, chocolate fountain machines, floral foam, tablecloth clips, Wilton candy melts

LiveAuctioneers.com
Aggregator of estate auctions, amazing for discontinued china patterns, vintage linens

Pastry Shops:
(favorite sources and places to visit if you're in the vicinity)

CARISSA'S BAKERY
(Long Island, NY)
carissasthebakery.com
For the meringue chocolate cake, the bouchons, honey oat loaf

CRAFTSMAN & WOLVES
(San Francisco, CA)
craftsman-wolves.com
For the Rebel Within, pâtes des fruits, all seasonal items

DELICIAS CUBAN BAKERY
(Palm Beach, FL)
deliciasbakeries.com
For guava pastries

THE KNEADED BREAD
(Port Chester, NY)
kneadedbread.com
For the brioches au sucre, chocolate bread, onions rolls

LULU'S BAKERY
(Scarsdale, NY)
everythinglulu.com
For the black & white cookies and occasion cakes

SOURCES OF CHEFANIE TABLEWARE

THE CHATHAM HOME
(Cape Code, MA)
thechathamhome.com

CHEFANIE
chefanie.com

THE GREY PEARL
(New York, NY)
thegreypearl.com

FESTE
(New York, NY)
lovefeste.com

FIFINELLA
(Abilene, TX)
shopfifinella.com

FRESH I.D.
(Little Rock, AK)
shopfreshid.com

JILL ROBERTS
(Los Angeles, CA)
jillroberts.com

THE KEMBLE SHOP
(Palm Beach, FL)
thekembleshop.com

KOIBIRD
(London, UK)
koibird.com

MADISON
(Dallas, TX)
madison214.com

MAMAN
(Auckland, NZ)
maman.co.nz

MANSE
(Alexandria, VA)
shopmanse.com

NELLIE GEORGE
(Richmond, VA)
shopnelliegeorge.com

PALOMA & CO
(Houston, TX)
shoppalomaandco.com

PLATE & PEONIE
(Bombay, India)
plateandpeonie.com

PRISM
(Seattle, WA)
prismseattle.com

SUNSET & CO
(San Antonio, TX)
sunsetandco.com

Acknowledgments

There are so many people to thank for making the brand and this book come to life.

Immense thanks to Stockton Johnson, Collins Nai, Yumi Matsuo, and Quentin Bacon for the colorful, vivid photographs that leap from the pages.

Eternal gratitude to my team of Julia Munhoz, Tiffany Youdim, Molly Kaplan Krueger, Kim Cressman, and everyone else who has passed through. I could not have done this without you, your boundless talents, and your giant smiles.

I'm indebted to event partners who made so many of these chapters possible, including Carter Johnston, Leatherology, Inn at Perry Cabin, Waterdrinker Farms, PatBo, Cara Cara, LoveShackFancy, Rebecca Hessel Cohen, and Charlotte Brody.

Rozanne Gold—thank you for your mentorship and encouragement.

Meg Thompson, book agent extraordinaire—thank you for believing in this book when it was just a conversation, and thank you for matching me with the perfect team.

The amazing Rizzoli team of Kathleen Jayes, Doug Turshen, David Huang, and Tricia Levi—thank you for holding me to the highest standards and then pushing me further. You taught me so much, and I appreciate your endless patience along the way. It has been such a privilege to work with you.

Finally, I thank my family and friends who have been the source of inspiration and motivation since the very beginning. I wouldn't be half the cook I am without constantly wanting to impress you. Mom and Dad—thank you for cultivating all of this in your home and kitchen. Grandpa, Teddy, Jessy, Jack, Daryn, Christie, Cassius, Jack, Alara, Paige, and David—thank you for all the gathering. I love you the most.

First published in the United States of America
in 2024 by
Rizzoli International Publications, Inc.
300 Park Avenue South
New York, NY 10010
www.rizzoliusa.com

All photos by Stockton Johnson except:

Quentin Bacon: 34, 45, 46, 49, 55, 57, 59, 67, 77, 78, 79, 120, 127, 128, 129, 131, 136, 138, 140, 141, 148, 151, 152, 153

Rommel Demano: 98, 100, 102

Camila Giraldo: 25, 34, 40, 41, 149, 226, 227, 231

Jordan Hanna: 26, 34, 73, 74, 75, 76, 80, 81

Andrew Katzowitz for Ann Taylor: 29

Katie Kosaya for The International Culinary Center: 24

Yumi Matsuo for Guest of a Guest: 9, 10

Kate Milford: 11

Collins Nai: 6, 12, 14, 15, 20, 21, 23, 30, 34, 51, 52, 53, 54, 56, 84, 87, 88, 89, 91, 92

Kristina Nameless: 180, 217, 218, 220

Stephanie Nass: 5, 32–33, 150, 235

Sofia Sanchez-Zarate: 64, 69

Emily Schindler: 31, 44, 47

Scott Suchman: 120, 133, 134, 135, 137, 139, 228, 229, 231, 233

Molly Tavoletti for Fancy Peasant: 25

Nick Tininenko for Snow Lodge: 34, 37, 38, 39, 42, 43, 48

Publisher: Charles Miers
Senior Editor: Kathleen Jayes
Copyeditor: Tricia Levi
Design by Doug Turshen with David Huang
Production Manager: Kaija Markoe
Managing Editor: Lynn Scrabis

Printed in China

2024 2025 2026 2027 / 10 9 8 7 6 5 4 3 2 1

ISBN: 978-0-8478-2943-9
Library of Congress Control Number: 2024934782

Visit us online:
Facebook.com/RizzoliNewYork
Twitter: @Rizzoli_Books
Instagram.com/RizzoliBooks
Pinterest.com/RizzoliBooks
Youtube.com/user/RizzoliNY
Issuu.com/Rizzoli